Mindfulness
in Sound

OTHER TITLES IN THIS SERIES:

The Art of Mindful Baking

The Art of Mindful Birdwatching

The Art of Mindful Gardening

The Art of Mindful Reading

The Art of Mindful Silence

The Art of Mindful Singing

The Art of Mindful Walking

Einstein and the Art of Mindful Cycling

Galileo and the Art of Ageing Mindfully

Happiness and How it Happens

The Heart of Mindful Relationships

The Joy of Mindful Writing

The Mindful Art of Wild Swimming

The Mindful Man

Mindful Crafting

Mindful Pregnancy and Birth

Mindful Travelling

Mindfulness and Compassion

Mindfulness and Music

Mindfulness and Surfing

Mindfulness and the Art of Drawing

Mindfulness and the Art of Managing Anger

Mindfulness and the Art of Urban Living

Mindfulness and the Journey of Bereavement

Mindfulness and the Natural World

Mindfulness at Work

Mindfulness for Black Dogs and Blue Days

Mindfulness for Students

Mindfulness for Unravelling Anxiety

The Mindfulness in Knitting

The Practice of Mindful Yoga

Zen and the Path of Mindful Parenting

Mindfulness
in Sound

Tune in to the world around us

Mark Tanner

Leaping Hare Press

First published in the UK and North America in 2020 by

Leaping Hare Press

An imprint of The Quarto Group
The Old Brewery, 6 Blundell Street
London N7 9BH, United Kingdom
T (0)20 7700 6700
www.QuartoKnows.com

Text © 2020 Mark Tanner
Design and layout © 2020 Quarto Publishing plc

All rights reserved. No part of this book may be reproduced
or transmitted in any form or by any means, electronic or mechanical, including
photocopying, recording, or by any information storage and retrieval system,
without written permission from the copyright holder.

British Library Cataloguing-in-Publication Data
A catalogue record for this book is available from the British Library

ISBN: 978-1-78240-997-7

This book was conceived, designed and produced by

Leaping Hare Press

58 West Street, Brighton BN1 2RA, United Kingdom
Publisher DAVID BREUER
Art Director JAMES LAWRENCE
Editorial Director TOM KITCH
Commissioning Editor MONICA PERDONI
Project Editor JOANNA BENTLEY
Design Manager ANNA STEVENS
Designer GINNY ZEAL
Illustrator MELVYN EVANS

Printed in China

1 3 5 7 9 10 8 6 4 2

CONTENTS

Introduction 6

CHAPTER ONE
Sound as Meditation 22

CHAPTER TWO
Pathways to Sound 50

CHAPTER THREE
Meditation Sounded Out 70

CHAPTER FOUR
Deep Listening 92

CHAPTER FIVE
The Sound of Speech 102

CHAPTER SIX
Soundscapes 118

Resources 140
Index 141
Dedication & Acknowledgements 144

INTRODUCTION

*Sound unites us all. And yet, sound is only
real for those with ears to hear it. Every sound
needs an attentive listener, or it's as if it's not
happening, like a small child pirouetting beautifully
in a park, unobserved by anyone else. Sound is a
symptom of something physical that is occurring, or
has already occurred, whether this be a bird pecking at
a nut or its echo reverberating down an alleyway. Once
we've become receptive, sound instantly switches to
being something unmistakably vivid, yet seconds earlier
it had passed us by unnoticed. When sound and
meditation intertwine, our journey
into mindfulness begins.*

YOUR PERSONAL JOURNEY THROUGH SOUND

◆

Sound is detonating all around us. And in between, we have the blessing of silence, less commonly found but equally beautiful. Though sound mostly comes to us free of charge, its capacity to inform us, move us and stir us into action is priceless.

SOUND, LIKE LIGHT, HAS LIMITLESS FREQUENCIES, and with it an inexhaustible capacity for stirring our emotions. Just as white light is a spectrum of colours that have come together as one, white noise is where every conceivable sound frequency converges into a constant, ambient sound. Though white noise, such as air conditioning, can aid sleep or block out a loud voice nearby, it can also be a valuable tool for meditation. But mindfulness is not about pretending the world is without its distractions; we can learn to harness sound, in all its complexity and mystical power, so that we become more focused, aware and alive to the moment.

Without perhaps realizing it, our environment continually resonates, buzzes and chimes, however aloof or distant from its source we may be. But all this eager hullabaloo is easily squandered if our ears lag behind its beat. When we spot something happening nearby, we instinctively turn our eyes in its direction, raise an eyebrow, tilt our head to sharpen our focus. But noticing doesn't need to be a visual response; it can equally be auditory. The echo of a door slamming will comfortably outlive the nanosecond it took us to watch it happen. A fanfare of car horns tells us more in a split second than staring fixedly at a row of taxis inching their way down a gridlocked street. And the sound of a waterfall will live on in the aural memory far more vividly than its mental photo-graph. For this reason, we may recognize a human voice many years after we last heard it – even a voice that might to others seem unremarkable. Its distinctive timbre seeps into our sub-conscious and could be ready to return to us in an instant, just when we least expect it.

We commonly speak of overlooking something – not seeing it, or else not seeing its value – and yet this presupposes it is our capacity for sight that has been allowed to lapse. For a person practised in mindfulness on the other hand, sound – or perhaps the very absence of it – amounts to more than a personal sensation playing itself out somewhere in the brain; it is the medium through which meditation most easily begins. This is why Buddhists use bells to help them meditate – not to dull the senses, but to draw their minds deeper and closer to their spirituality.

Being alert to sound is the easiest thing in the world, yet we so quickly take it for granted. The more amorphous and flowing a sound is, the more helpful it will be when it comes to harnessing our breathing, slowing down our private world and becoming aware of each passing nanosecond. It can almost seem that time itself has its own distinctive sound.

FINDING YOUR INNER POINT OF RESONANCE

We may think we can see a sound source because of its influence on a nearby physical object, such as a table vibrating on a moving train or a marquee buffeted in a gale. But the sensation of hearing a sound is not the sound itself, nor is observing with our eyes the effect of whatever it was that created the sound.

WE OFTEN SAY THAT SOMETHING 'resonates with us', 'strikes a chord' or 'rings a bell', when what we really mean is that we sense a connection beyond what may be visible or audible to others around us. Whether in response to a sound or not, this goes further than déjà vu; it may feel otherworldly or purely instinctive – and then, just like the sound of breaking glass, it's gone again in an instant.

Resonance itself is real, measurable and quantifiable, the stuff of physics students and sound scientists, the currency of acousticians, noise pollution measurers and analysts of a dozen kinds besides, not to mention the lifeblood of musicians, racing car drivers, comedians and dance instructors. Vibrations are sounds that can be sensed in ways other than through the ears, though of course we frequently feel and hear vibrations simultaneously and are barely aware they are being filtered through different senses simultaneously. In much the same way, we combine the taste and smell of a piece of cake as we fold it into our mouth, delighting in how it melts on our tongue. We could temporarily suspend one or more of these senses and still gain a great deal from the ones we are left with. This may also explain why I enjoy the taste of the Asian fruit, durian, but find myself retching at its odour; even more bizarrely perhaps, I adore the taste of oysters, but feel queasy at the very thought of their texture. To an extent, I find I can switch off undesirable characteristics and focus on the ones that give me pleasure. For me, a chilled Easter egg comes as close to perfection as I can get in terms of a synergy of all five senses: its tactility, curvaceous form and crisp shattering sound adds immeasurably to its taste and aroma.

Real or Perceived Sounds

We could become aware of a sound source without actually hearing it, for example, when we feel the vibration of a door bell but cannot hear it ring in the apartment above. Or we could begin to notice a sound we ourselves created without realizing it, such as water trickling from an overfilled plant pot. We resonate both physically in our ears when we hear, but also internally, to the imagined or remembered emotions we associate with previously heard sounds. We know that it's possible to measure what happens in someone's brain when they are subjected to a sound source, or perhaps more interestingly, when given a prompt that triggers an imagined sound reaction. Perhaps such 'non-existent' resonances might even be picked up by someone else whose perception is sufficiently tuned in? In an atomically tiny way, it seems to me something of the *actual* sound must exist in order for it to be imagined: from the metaphysical to the physical, virtually undetected, like a magician's sleight of hand. For these reasons, perceived sound is possibly more intriguing than 'real' sound, even from my privileged vantage point as a professional musician. Indeed, for a musician, internalized music can gradually take over to a point where one switches from real sounds to imagined ones as effortlessly as a bilingual person diverts from one language to another mid-sentence.

What our physical brain does when processing sound should matter less to us than the fanciful dance that is playing itself out continually in our imagination. Ultimately it is this that becomes meaningful and enduring. I'm not talking about the soundtrack to our lives that stultifies the natural flow of life itself, but the spontaneous sparks of sound that illuminate us and then leave us alone again, like the waft of coconut oil on a beach, or the unexpectedly sensual touch of a dog's nose on our fingers. This is the point where the quantifiable aspects of sound reveal themselves as having only limited value for us as human beings – the notion that if it's not measurable it's not *there* is nothing short of a catastrophic underestimation of sound in terms of how it touches us. Somehow, it's as though sound is connected to us more fundamentally than the visual. A vibration from one thing to another, or especially from one person to another, is a transference of something tangible –

we know it to be *real* – yet this is only in the crudest sense explainable through physics. Whether it's the shrill rasp of a bird, the stuttering trickle of water down a rusty drainpipe or the afternoon-long coverage of a sports match, it will be the sound that we want to draw that little bit more closely into ourselves and that we remember and learn from.

Our inner point of resonance can prove tantalisingly elusive, and retracing the path to it may not be easy even five minutes later. For we will soon enough likely have become distracted by some other sound that came to us only because we happened to be sitting where we were at that precise moment. Reassuringly though, an oft-repeated sound can eventually become so familiar that it triggers a process of accessing this precious innermost place. Sound, real or imagined, can become an indispensable catalyst to self-awareness and our sense of time and place. Noticing our sound environment is a first step towards repurposing it for future meditation, or giving us another point of resonance between ourselves and the world around us.

An ability to tap into natural sound opens up an aural vista of possibilities for self-awareness and inner serenity. This book will help you to do this through a process of active engagement and submission to the beauty of sound; it will encourage you to build a compelling soundscape for yourself whenever you wish to, simply by drawing from the sound readily available around you.

The Healing Power of Sound

The medicinal and restorative qualities of sound have been harnessed effectively in Tibetan Buddhist rituals for many centuries. The sounds made by Tibetan singing bowls are said to be able to restore whichever parts of the body, mind or soul have become temporarily misaligned. This type of 'energy medicine', or 'sound medicine' has an unmistakable allure, not just for Buddhists but for any of us who feel we have lost our inner vigour. The word 'entrainment' is used to describe a method of realignment, or the re-establishing of a person's brainwaves in precise resonance with a certain frequency. It might be helpful to be aware of what the word means in other contexts.

A dip in a person's energy flow can be remedied by closer synchrony with sound

In biomusicology, entrainment means 'the synchronization of organisms to an external rhythm', whereas in chronobiology (concerned with cyclical physiological phenomena), it is 'the alignment of a circadian system's period and phase to an external rhythm'. In hydrodynamics, entrainment is 'the movement of one fluid by another', while in physics, it means 'the process whereby two interacting oscillating systems assume the same period'. Finally, in the field of 'lexical entrainment' (concerned with words and their use within a language), it means 'the process in conversational linguistics of the subject adopting the terms of their interlocutor' – or in simpler words, where ambiguity is overcome by reaching a kind of 'conceptual agreement'. In all of these contexts, spiritual or biological, a broad theme can be seen: a purposeful attempt to reunite two or more elements which have, for whatever reason, lost their point of mutual orientation.

Sound might bring us closer to a more spiritual interpretation of entrainment through *vibration* – feeling a vibration run through our body, coupled with hearing it with our ears. By allowing a particular sound, such as Tibetan singing bowls, to touch us at an emotional level, we can use it to flatten out any irregularities of our body or mental state. It is the unique sonorities of these bowls that can, it is claimed by leading sound-healing experts, impact on all aspects of our daily lives. Used with chanting, as we shall see later, some feel that we can become more relaxed, feel less inhibited or weighed down by the stresses and strains of life.

The concept of 'dis-ease' being likened to 'disease' is certainly intriguing and at least to some extent logical and demonstrable. Some practitioners who use singing bowls are of the opinion that a point of natural, unfettered resonance can ultimately be reached, and that a dip in a person's energy flow can be remedied by closer synchrony with the sound. If we imagine an unhealthy aspect of ourselves as being out of kilter with the rest of us, its qualities of vibration will cease to flow as easily. Speaking for myself, certain sounds elevate my consciousness transformation more than others, and I wouldn't claim any consistency, either to my ability to enter this state of resonance or to benefit from it, but there are certainly times when sound therapy is of heightened value.

The Healing Power of Laughter

The sound of laughter is conducive to mindfulness because it is something we experience impulsively and reflect outwardly in the moment. Laughter tugs us gently from feelings of discontent and tension, permits us to focus more clearly on what really matters in our lives and equips us to move forward with renewed vigour and enthusiasm.

We all like a good laugh. A well-timed moment of levity can go a long way to alleviating a humdrum day, and a smile easily tips into a laugh with a little encouragement. Though comedians will tell you they may need to modify their humour to accommodate different nationalities, a giggle in French is perhaps not so different from a chuckle in Spanish or a guffaw in German. Laughter brings us together as we learn to share common ground, however briefly. Laughter has astonishing powers we might not have imagined. For example, did you know that a good laugh can actually build up your immune system, reduce physical pain and alleviate mental disorders, stress and tension?

The sound of an unrestrained fit of laughter is infectious; it beckons us to bond even more joyously with those we love, and at the same time nudges us to become better acquainted with those we have only just met. When we were children, the slightest indiscretion or faux pas was immediately used as a vehicle for an outburst of cacophonous laughter. Even those things that perhaps ought not to have seemed funny somehow were, such as someone tripping on a loose paving stone, or an unguarded breaking of wind in the quiet confines of the class-room. And at the other end of our life, when the strain of physical and mental impairments can seem to have conspired against us, the sound of laughter will often return like a long-lost friend to remind us that there is still a value to our existence. Laughter distracts us from the aches and pains of our joints, and there is some evidence to suggest that the positive effects of a side-splitting laugh can reverberate for up to an hour after.

We should aim to savour and value the irresistible sound of laughter and its contagious qualities more readily in our lives, simply because life is best lived in an atmosphere of joy.

Streams of Consciousness

Water shares persuasive similarities with human life. The steady, assured trickle of a babbling brook is not unlike the blood coursing through our veins. Its sense of travel, of motion towards somewhere uncertain, parallels the ebb and flow of our years; vigorous and brimming with optimism at the start, yet becoming more measured and selective in its route as it contemplates more complex terrain. The sound water makes, whether buffeted charismatically against a rugged coastline or as it congregates pensively in a rock pool, mirrors our emotional response to life. And, just as sand is the natural consequence of water patiently cutting through rock, we too wear the scars and laughter lines of our brief existence.

Bathed in Sound

The sound of a running bath is like an overture to a sprawling symphony – it begins with intermittent, anticipatory spurts of sound; chaotic, ricocheting and reverberant in its auditorium-like void. From here, a deeper tranche of sound slowly begins to form, as if to cushion the downpour from the taps, each of which has suddenly become more confident in their respective roles. Who knows what journey you will take as you relinquish your grip on the to-do list that has been pestering you since breakfast?

Before too long, other acoustical properties seem to be contributing – the coppery harmonics of pipes in full service, barely able to contain the upward surge of watery power; the kettle-like whistle that emits like a crazed hyena from the hot supply struggling to honour its obligations; the percussive interjections of soap dishes being tactically repositioned. By now, we have the makings of an impressive orchestral out-pouring – 'water music' of unrivalled passion and exuberance. A close-up slow-motion replay of your bath at this crucial stage in its evolution might resemble Niagara Falls, as all the elements collide together in a triumphant maelstrom. New tones now creep into the sound texture, such as the fizz of bath salts or the lining up of potions and perfumes for use later in this glorious ritual.

With a little ingenuity, a bath can become quite an acceptable mobile office; you just need access to hand-drying materials, something to drink, a phone or tablet and maybe an apple to stave off the nibbles if you've really planned well. I find the entire process of enjoying a bath mindful, from the optimistic preamble of assembling towels, clothes and soaps, to the moment an hour or more later when I emerge, pristinely clean and ready to meet all upcoming challenges with newfound vigour.

The sound of a running bath is like an overture to a sprawling symphony

The whole process of sinking down into my luxurious water chamber is for me a kind of giving-up, or giving-in at least; an opportunity to move from the reality of the day's work ahead of me, or else the tasks achieved earlier, into a precious, fabulous time warp. A bath is a place of sanctity, and yet at the same time a gateway to another place, where earthly preoccupations are suddenly subservient to timeless tranquillity. I imagine each section of my bath to be a little like turning over a new chapter of a book; allowing a limb to rise up from the depths seems to trigger a new emotional mini-journey, relishing the gentle sounds of water splashing and lapping as I move.

Make your bathing experience a thing of pure joy, worthy of every minute you can give to it. There is little expediency to a bath – yet any wastefulness of water is surely offset by the time you have yourself contributed to making it a valuable and memorable one. I like to lie in the bath for at least ten minutes after I've drained it. Hearing gravity suck the last residue of water south from underneath me is like experiencing the bath snore its deepest, most profound sleep. Bathing, whether alone or with a loved one, is a truly magical time with its own distinctive array of sounds that form an intrinsic and essential part of the experience. It's an invigorating intertwining of body and soul, an opportunity to journey the mind, to meditate and briefly lose contact with terra firma. Your bath is more a time machine, a vessel for sound that is always waiting to be set into motion.

MINDFULNESS EXERCISE

THAT RINGS A BELL

Meditation through silence is for many the preferred, or even the only way. Silence – or more accurately a noiseless environment – can minimize intrusiveness and hence reduce our tendency to tell ourselves 'stories', revisit past anxieties and, perhaps worst of all, plan things or mull over the possibilities that are impatiently lining up ahead of us.

But even an absence of noise can never be a guarantee we will stay focused on our meditation indefinitely. A solution to this is to set a timer to 'ding' unobtrusively at certain intervals, simply to prompt us back into a more conducive state of mind and snuff out the inclination to recall and cogitate. You might download a suitably discreet sound from the internet to use for such timely punctuations, or else record meditation 'cycles' in less regular or predictable units of time – when I first tried this with exact five-minute interval markers I realized I was tending to calculate inwardly the passing of time, which of course is the very opposite of being mindful! So, you could create a noiseless track with ever-widening time intervals between your preferred sound-marker, or alternatively, if you find it difficult to remain focused for even the shortest time, create a track which has progressively shorter interval markers.

The types of sound you might use will be entirely personal to you of course, but why not invest in some Tibetan Ting-Sha bells? Striking the rim of a tall glass partly filled with water, using a pencil or other non-metallic 'beater', can be just as effective. Finally, you might experiment with complementing some of your more successful homemade nature-sound meditation tracks with time-markers, so that you get the best of both worlds.

CHAPTER ONE

SOUND AS MEDITATION

*Breathing is the sound of us existing. It's
what helps us experience a temporal resonance
with life. Listening to — or 'watching' — your breathing
isn't about affecting an ostentatious influx and out-
flux of air, it's simply about choosing to be more aware,
more present. Conscious breathing shouldn't be hard
work or something that leaves us 'out' of breath, but
a way by which we can regulate and interweave
the physical and metaphysical.*

THE WISDOM OF BREATHING

◆

Because we don't need to think about breathing, quite often we don't. And when we neglect to connect regularly with our breathing, we easily lose track of the value it has for us. Instead, be mindful of your breathing; breathe in, and know you are breathing in; breathe out, and know you are breathing out.

I F WE HAD TO THINK ABOUT EVERY BREATH we take, we'd soon keel over. Thankfully, the medulla, which sits at the base of the brain where it connects to the spinal cord, takes care of primary functions of this sort, also heart beating, swallowing and blood pressure regulation. The sound we make when we breathe isn't something many of us are drawn to, and it can be distracting to be in close proximity to a noisy snorer or someone whose adenoids seem hyperactive.

Something extraordinary and invigorating seems to happen when we do this simplest of things: *just breathe*. The process of filling your lungs is nourishment for the brain, while breathing out is like your brain releasing its grip on anything that's threatening it through tension, anxiety or hostility. This is why breathing is just as important when releasing as when inhaling. Even though exhaling is the body's way of giving up spent air, it also has value for us in terms of emphasizing a connection to time and place. We could think of this as the folds and ripples of the sea as it meets the shore, or the

creaking motion to and fro we experience when lying in a hammock against the warm breeze of a sultry evening. Breathing isn't a skill, as such, and yet it most certainly improves with practice. Importantly, we are not practising breathing, but practising *noticing* our breathing. For me, breathing is the sound of time itself passing through me like grains of sand in the thinnest of downward streams.

If you put your fingers in your ears you will instantly hear your breathing more vividly – I like to wear headphones on aeroplanes, not often to listen to music, but simply to give me the sensation of my breathing as it reaffirms my sense of now. Slowing down your breathing has a calming effect, which in turn seems to activate a new dimension to your thinking. You could imagine the space between exhaling and inhaling as a kind of timeless subconsciousness. It's the point of temporary relaxation where the body is truly relieved of all its duties.

Think of breathing in and out as the folds and ripples of the sea as it meets the shore

The wisdom of breathing lies in its simplicity and in the time it takes to do it. As we tune in to the sound of our breathing, we learn to savour the sense of stillness our body has established on its own behalf. The autopilot breathing we do for the rest of our waking hours, I like to think, then becomes that little bit more measured and at ease with itself.

MINDFULNESS EXERCISE

SOUND ADVICE

An increased awareness of the sounds all around us can lead to a height-ened sense of now. Because it takes us *time* to absorb what we are hearing, we become more present, more conscious of each living moment.

Sit in a place where you won't be disturbed and simply *be* for a while. At first, allow your eyes to move slowly in the plane they most conveniently find themselves – don't be in a hurry to make sense of your surroundings. Close your eyes and take your breathing on a slow journey through your mind; let it flow like oil over the craggy surfaces out on the distant land-scape, rise up to the summit of the highest tree, or become so light that you move as gracefully as any hot-air balloon. Allow your breathing to become a living thing.

It hardly matters what sound you hear first, it may well not be there for long enough to be intelligible. Should your mind try to penetrate the sound, give yourself permission not to. Resist categorizing the sounds, be governed by the intrigue and beauty of the sound itself, its direct impact or impression. If this proves tricky, slowly move your mind to the spaces – even if they are not really *silences* – that permeate your soundscape. By moving unhurriedly between the sounds and the spaces in between, our breathing will appear to take the form of a fluid, continually moving organism.

Stretch out each passing sound as if it were made of elastic. If a sound repeats itself, let it do so. Your sound meditation can take on the value of a power nap, leaving you feeling rejuvenated and ready to reopen your eyes. Move on more purposefully through your day, taking brief moments to reconnect with the sensation of sound you enjoyed earlier.

There's Always More to Hear

When parking my car outside a supermarket the other day, I yanked on the handbrake with a little greater vigour than I normally would. It was a hot day, so my window was fully rolled down. The noise of the ratchet on the brake echoed across the fairly empty concrete space surrounding me, and two seconds later, as I emerged from the car, I heard a remarkably similar sound come back at me from perhaps twenty yards away. I knew immediately it was some kind of bird, but I couldn't tell you what. I smiled to myself as I ambled silently towards the shopping trollies stacked together like sardine tins, and then stopped in my tracks. I had to know if I was right, that this had been a form of conversation, so I turned on my heels and got back in my car, leaving the door open and reapplying the handbrake just as before. Sure enough, my newly acquainted bird obliged with its oddly effective mimicking noise. For the rest of that day I found myself looking out for similar chance exchanges of sound – a mobile ringtone that resembled a door bell as someone walked past a house, or a cough resembling a shopping bag being stuffed into the boot of a van. If this random bird had brought a smile to my face, presumably the bird knew it was communicating with me? There's always more to hear.

I had a similar experience recently when foraging for berries. Berry picking is an art form, and yet the main attributes required are stealthy diligence, an ability to keep your centre

MINDFULNESS EXERCISE

WATER YOUR PLANTS

For me, there can be fewer more pleasurable things to do on a balmy early summer's evening than drench plants in more water than they could possibly need. The more I give them, the more fulfilled I feel. Perhaps the thanks they give me for these nocturnal acts of generosity are entirely imagined, or simply a case of me giving myself what I crave? Watering plants is mindful in so many ways – you are communing with nature, distancing yourself from the distractions of the moment, and at the same time, sharing sustenance. As you move from plant to plant, you revisit a pattern not wholly unfamiliar to you; it's a kind of ultra-slow dance. If you don't have a garden, perhaps you have space to assemble a small yet beautiful collection of house plants, bonsai or cacti? Sit back and enjoy your handiwork as you listen to the *drip, drip, drip* of life itself.

of gravity while standing on tiptoe, and a willingness to tolerate the odd scratch and sting. A spontaneous desire to reach in for a single plump berry when sauntering down a country lane easily turns into a forty-minute practical meditation in which the pursuit of fruit, tantalizingly out of reach, becomes a tale of derring-do to impress the family as you proudly present your hatful of fruit. A word of advice at this point – bury the fattest examples under the more diminutive ones if you've any ambition for a pie that evening.

As I wandered inch by inch down the same narrow lane a week later, a small crow supervised from its ideal vantage point on a nearby wall. I interpreted its occasional snippets of song as helpful clues to where the most voluptuous berries were hidden beneath the nettles and bramble foliage. I found myself nodding in agreement and even responding in kind with a sort of bird-whistle, intelligible only to him and me. Clearly this odd banter had some sort of basis for meaningful communication if my brimming bowl of berries was anything to go by. 'Don't forget to look low as well as high,' he prompted me; my war wounds are proof that I listened and responded enthusiastically to his nudging, for I had more than enough berries to keep the family reaching for more pie.

20/20 HEARING

Perfect sight has never been part of the 'design brief' for any animal — humans included. We can only make the best use of what our bodies have evolved to do, be it fending off attack from the rear, or pinpointing potential prey from high up on a cliff.

WE REFER TO 20/20 *VISION* ALL THE TIME, commonly to describe someone's exceptional powers of sight. We might even use it pejoratively, for example 'twenty-twenty hindsight is a wonderful thing', meaning that being wise after the event is a good deal easier than when forced to make the

right call in the moment. But actually, most sighted people have 20/20 vision – the term simply means that from a distance of twenty feet a person can see as clearly as we'd expect them to be able to. On the other hand, an optometrist would be quick to point out that there are other components which contribute to a human being's optimal sightedness, such as how well our peripheral vision functions, whether our focus and colour recognition is good, how well our eyes are coordinated and sharply focused, also how quickly these various attributes can typically align themselves in a variety of real-world situations.

Our near-distance sightedness might easily outstrip our long sight, for example, or of course vice versa. In any case, none of us has 'perfect' vision, not compared to animals that possess especially clear long-distance sight, for example, such as owls. Perfect sight means different things to different living creatures, and few have evolved to incorporate more than one or two of the attributes I will sketch out here. For example, there's a bizarre-looking creature called the mantis shrimp (which literally has eyes on stalks) that has appreciably better vision than we do. A goat's eyes bulge out from the sides of its head so far that it can practically see all around it (about 50 per cent more than us humans in the horizontal plane). A falcon has a truly impressive long-distance sight, which it regularly calls upon when scanning for prey and soaring at higher altitudes.

Hearing Range

So, is there an equivalent to 20/20 vision in hearing? There's certainly a 'normal' bandwidth as regards volume perception, measured in decibels – we can detect a range of approximately 120 dB, and all the shades in between, covering the quietest to loudest sounds. But because of the ways our ears have evolved to make sense of volume, it takes ten times the power of a sound to register as having doubled, which means that ten people shouting at once will appear only twice as loud as one person. This also explains what we might think of as the opposite scenario – it can be incredibly difficult to blot out undesirable sounds – if we eliminate 99 per cent of a sound source, leaving just 1 per cent remaining, we will still be able to hear 80 per cent of it. What's more, a change in volume of less than 1 db, whether higher or lower, won't be detectable at all. So, put in simplified terms, there is the *actual* volume at which a sound occurs in our environment, and our *perceived* volume. The difference is sometimes called 'exponential', measured on a logarithmic scale.

To some extent, the way our ears deal with an excess of sound must be a function of our evolved place in the world, as well as the world's own evolution – had we evolved in an even noisier world, with volcanoes perpetually erupting or unimaginable thunder storms kicking off for hours every day, presumably the gap between real and perceived sound would have needed to be greater, else we'd all be deaf! 'Normal'

volume levels for human beings are not usually challenged by the natural environment, or if they are (such as would be the case if standing near to a waterfall or earthquake) we can usually escape to somewhere calmer. But we are of course more than capable of wrecking our own hearing by listening to excessively loud music or working without protection with noisy machinery. Normal volume for speech is roughly 60 dB SPL (SPL means 'sound power level', linked to the logarithmic scale just mentioned), and noise levels are said to be harmful to the human ear at over 140 dB (SPL).

How Our Ears Work

The visible outer part of the human ear, along with the ear canal (at the end of which the all-important tympanic membrane is stretched), is an elaborate mechanism that does the initial job of channelling or directing an external sound deep into the head. The intricate organs known as the middle ear (comprised of a tiny lattice of bones) and inner ear (the cochlea, a snail-shaped, liquid-filled tube) are what we might call the 'business end' of our hearing. First, an external sound wave will set in motion the vibrating membrane, and from here a complex process of decoding occurs before we can begin to make sense of it in terms of pitch (or frequency – i.e. how high or low a sound presents itself to us), where it comes from (this is by far the weakest aspect of our hearing) and timbre (the specific tone we associate with a sound source,

whether this happens to be a wardrobe being dragged across a stone floor or a musical instrument such as a bassoon, which could have vaguely similar frequencies). In terms of frequency, our overall range of hearing is roughly 20 Hz to 20 kHz (aha! 20/20 hearing!) though our most refined hearing range is between 1 and 4 kHz.

Of particular note is the level of sensitivity at which our ears can detect sound when dealing with the quietest levels. It has been observed in sound laboratories that the physical resonance motion of the eardrum is barely that of a single molecule when our hearing is functioning at this most quiet level. This would suggest that our hearing, as well as our most acute sensitivity to sound in other ways, functions much better at these quietest levels, and moreover that our levels of stress could be adversely affected by continually pushing the boundaries of our hearing, especially as regards volume. The notion of tranquillity, both inwardly and outwardly, would therefore appear to have a scientific as well as spiritual basis.

The fact that we have two ears is significant for a number of reasons, not simply because we can have double the amount of volume intensity entering our heads at one time. Perhaps the most important of these is that we can better gauge the *direction* from which a sound source is coming. This happens because our brain can detect an incredibly small variation in distance from the source to each ear (there will commonly be such a difference, and we can detect this even when only three

degrees apart), and hence the brain is able to compute this a little like coordinates on a satnav. The ear furthest away senses an infinitesimal delay in arrival of the sound compared to the ear closest to it. The physical distance between the ears also allows us to pick up the subtlest *volume* difference – the ear nearer to the sound source will hear it as being louder, and the other as quieter. As we continually move our heads, we are forever altering the sound signal to our brain in these two planes – volume intensity and time delay – and this gives an ever-altering fix on the sound. This explains why a monaural sound played through headphones will appear to be coming from a point midway in our head; it also helps explain how a skilled sound engineer can simulate the positions of orchestral or band players using a technique called 'panning', adding to our enjoyment and sense of occasion.

When it comes to distance sound measuring, unlike a bat we have comparatively few clues to work with. Our brain seems hardwired to accept a higher-pitched sound as being nearer to us, simply because it is these higher frequencies which dribble away first over distance, so a low-pitched sound will more likely be interpreted as being far off, such as a roll of thunder, whereas a bird might be heard as nearer simply because it is higher. In addition, we subconsciously use echoes to gain an approximate sense of how far away a sound began its life. However, this is a somewhat crude and unreliable method compared with, say, a dolphin, which can send out a

MINDFULNESS EXERCISE

SHAPE WHAT YOU HEAR

It's an interesting experiment to fix on a particular sound and then block off your hearing to one ear – you may feel as if you are losing *more* than half of what you could hear with both ears in action, as well as introducing a 'new' sound. Further to this, try gently bending your ears out of shape (there are many weird and wonderful ways you might do this), either when you are listening to music or to someone talking on the radio. Doing this illustrates, albeit crudely, how important the specific shape of the outer ear is to our individual way of *perceiving* sound.

The next time you find yourself in a public swimming pool or a big church, close your eyes and see if you are able to distinguish between the noises happening close by and those occurring further away. The difficulty is that each sound source is not only coming from a different distance, but will be at a different volume, and the acoustical properties of the space won't be uniform either. What we hear is a kind of sound stew, with only barely discernible separation as our ears struggle to disentangle the different sounds.

click and detect how long it takes to receive it back again – an impressively sophisticated call and response mechanism which humans simply did not need to evolve in order to survive.

Besides volume and pitch, we have timbre, or tone quality. While arguably humans could to some extent survive satisfactorily without our extraordinary ability to perceive different

'The human voice is the most perfect instrument of all.'

ARVO PÄRT, COMPOSER

timbres, there can be little doubt life would be a whole lot less enjoyable. It would also be downright confusing, not to mention perilous, since the roar of a lion might be confused for a passing motor vehicle or bass guitar, and all people of the same sex we communicate with would sound very much the same. We'd still have useful clues of accent, volume, syntax, rhythm and pacing to help us distinguish one person from another, but without the subtle qualities of timbre we take for granted, sound would lack its identity-giving colour and individuality. Our world would become black and white, and our ability to engage with it would inevitably diminish. Not unlike music, it is those aspects of ordinary sound that we cannot conveniently convert into data that turn out to be the most character-giving and life-affirming. Everyday sounds are a bounty of such nuances, forever tumbling over each other, mutating and playing wonderful tricks with our psychology.

Life without tone is unimaginable to me. I'm guessing it might be a little like eating without a capacity to taste – leaving only an ability to assess a food by its texture, weight and temperature; after all, eating is so much more than a process we go through to ensure we live a few days longer. The timbre, or tone colour of a particular sound is specific to it, since for

each one an intricate interplay of variables in frequency, amplitude, overtones and harmonics give it a kind of finger-print. What we might think of as being one sound is really a mixture – just as the taste of a particular brand of strawberry jam is a complex mix of fruits, sugars, chemicals and other identity-giving characteristics that distinguish it from another brand. Two female voices speaking the same word at the same speed, volume and pitch will still be distinguishable from each other. Even the most advanced spectrogram cannot match the multitude of ways the human brain is instantly able to make sense of the all-important aspects of sound known as 'spectrum' and 'envelope', let alone the other variables of sound which give it its authenticity. Voice analysis experts still need to employ an amount of trained subjective decision-making in addition to computer enhancement and spectrum analysis software. This is because such software is essentially an attempt to produce a *visual* representation of sound, which by definition only has real meaning for us when we hear it. It seems likely that something intrinsic to the sound itself will always be lost in translation.

Deep Listening

An ability to detect sounds from far away, to be able to distin-guish precisely between different pitches and timbres, volumes and directions, are the attributes of fully functional hearing. These faculties are governed more by chance than

anything else – a person born with hearing impairments or reduced capacity in any of the areas just mentioned is therefore having to deal with, and possibly compensate for, aspects of their auditory machinery. *Listening*, on the other hand, is a facet of perception, how we attempt to make sense of sound, not just the amount or quality of it that makes it safely past the eardrum into the brain. To a variable extent, listening capabilities will inevitably be impacted on by hearing impediments. We cannot listen if we cannot hear, so it stands to reason that a smaller amount of sound will limit the information our brain has to work with.

In the realm of listening, a person can nevertheless excel even if they only possess moderate hearing. This is because unlike hearing, listening implies an amount of concentration and discernment. It also requires contextual understanding – an awareness of what the audible clues amount to. Listening can be a mindful activity because it is one of the ways we can improve our ability to take notice of what we are hearing. And when we notice, there is the possibility we will alter our behaviour. The act of listening might take advantage of information gleaned from other senses, such as sight, whereas hearing is solely determined by an aural receptivity to vibrations. Admittedly, there are people who can pick up vibrations by means other than the ears (Evelyn Glennie, the percussionist, for example), or in other ways are able to supplement the information gleaned from sound waves. But when listen-

ing, it is the meaning behind what is being communicated that is important, not the precision with which the sounds themselves are internalized.

Nor is deep listening solely to do with the accurate transference of information through words. It is how we can penetrate the sounds all around us more gainfully. Just as when we listen with care to what someone is saying we expand our capacity to learn from them (gauging also perhaps their body gestures, facial expressions etc.), when we listen deeply to everyday sounds, we pick up more of the finer subtleties that give them colour. Hearing is a quantifiable biological attribute, whereas listening is more a cultivated skill; and like any other, it can be improved with practice.

How, then, can our listening be mindful if it is effortful? For me, the answer lies in which state of mind we happen to be in. There are times when we may wish sound to be unobtrusive, or not there at all. But there are also times when we want the multidimensionality of our sound environment to rise up and consume us. We get to decide if we are ready to move from one mode of listening to the other. When listening for meditation we are taught to resist the desire to understand or compute what we hear; we are noticing rather than analysing, allowing the sound to wash over us in whatever way it will. When deep listening, however, we are painting our personal sound image with a smaller brush; our curiosity brings with it a more vivid sense of purpose.

MINDFULNESS EXERCISE

ONE MOMENT IN TIME

Imagine a moment stretched out to an hour. A moment of blissful serenity that hadn't existed until you laid claim to it, not weighed down by anticipation or obligation. It's a moment without a relationship to time, only to you. Time is one of your most precious possessions; let this moment be a timeless pearl in the oyster of your day. An ideal moment would be while you're queuing in a shop or waiting for a train. Close your eyes, or fix on something that is not likely to be moving. Now notice any noise that is contributing to the natural sound design – it's unlikely to be one-dimensional, more probably a jumble of overlapping sounds. Let these fold in together, so that your meditation won't continually be at risk of being distracted.

Abrupt noises – a tannoy or a suitcase scratching along the ground – are not part of a conspiracy to undermine your moment. When you feel calm and are no longer judging what is happening around you, feel free to latch onto one sound and give in to it. You're not trying to evaluate or compartmentalize it, but to give yourself a vehicle with which to journey through your moment of quiet repose. The noisier the place you're in, the quieter you can be inside yourself; the sound itself is unimportant. Imagine each second is like a droplet of water in the ocean of your mind, and the sound you've locked on to is like a surfboard with you on it, moving gracefully forwards. The sound, the motion and time itself have for this brief period all synergized. At some point, your moment – however long – will come to an end. No matter, for you, these minutes began as a single moment and could potentially have lasted for hours.

I find I can move between these two mindsets more quickly and easily than I was once able to. As a musician I've grown used to listening inquisitively one minute, but enjoying the uncomplicated beauty of rainfall or birdsong the next. I don't regard one mode of listening as being superior to the other, merely different. Our ears register the existence of sound without conscious effort, but to become alive to its mystical qualities, either as a trigger for mindfulness or to bring us closer to the wonderment of each passing moment, involves a more thoughtful approach.

ACOUSTICS

Galileo invited us to consider the workings of the mind in processing and understanding sound, beyond the mechanics of sound or the properties of spaces in which we encounter it. In doing so, how we think about sound changed forever.

ACOUSTICS IS A SUBDIVISION OF SOUND PHYSICS, the study of mechanical wave motion found in the air around us, but also occurring in other gases, liquids and solids. Whereas the study of sound and acoustics – or sonics – was in Pythagoras's time (in the sixth century BCE) confined to determining why it was that some musical sounds appear more agreeable to the human ear, it was Aristotle two centuries earlier who first alluded to sound in terms of wave motion. ·

The first in-depth treatise on acoustics for theatres would emerge from the hand of the Roman architect Vitruvius, who considered among other things the properties of echoes. The design of a large public space based upon not just the physical dimensions and proportions of sound but the human ear's receptivity to it must have seemed a daring, not to mention costly leap of faith. Vitruvius's groundbreaking ideas were what led to the now ubiquitous raked seating in halls, theatres and other auditoria, in which the rapid deterioration of sound can to an appreciable extent be mitigated.

In what became known as the Scientific Revolution, it was Galileo Galilei and Marin Mersenne in the early seventeenth century who first grasped the idea that a vibrating string – a 'sonorous body' – sends vibrations detected by the ear 'which the mind interprets as sound' (Galileo). This seemingly obvious pronouncement in fact marked a crucial turning point in the long, complex history of sound physics. Galileo had dared to imagine what occurs psychologically when the physiological attributes of sound are filtered in the tympanum of the ear.

We can think of any acoustical occurrence as governed by a rapid five-stage chain of events with 'cause' at one end and 'effect' at the other; in between, we have the generation, propagation and reception stages, which might be triggered by a variety of natural means (i.e. occurring in the natural world) or volitional (by design or intent). In a fluid, such as the air, wave propagation manifests itself as a pressure wave.

Both the generation and reception stages involve transduction, a kind of conversion process. Even the subtlest changes to ambient air pressure can often be detectable by the human ear, and it is through a measuring of frequencies – the primary means by which our ears make sense of sound – that we can be more precise about how high or low a sound is. The transduction process is perhaps most easily understood by looking at a conventional loudspeaker, which channels dedicated frequencies through devices known as tweeters (for higher frequencies) and woofers (for lower frequencies).

The number of cycles per second is what governs these detectable levels, the units being Hertz. Frequencies which exist above 20,000 Hz (or 20 MHz) are known as ultrasonic, while those below 20 Hz are called infrasonic. The entire frequency spectrum can be understood more helpfully by dividing it into these three sections: infrasonic, audible, ultrasonic. These are entirely notional, since they are constructed to help define the band of audible sound that we humans can hear. While dolphins and other animals are capable of emitting and detecting sounds well outside of our upper range (ultrasonic), scientists can measure earthquakes by taking account of extremely low frequencies (infrasonic).

There are countless fascinating ways by which acousticians might harness the complex subdisciplines of sound physics for practical purposes. These extend well beyond the more obvious established avenues, such as designing concert halls

with optimum efficiency, or refining stereo systems. Among these are spectrum analysis (a handy visual representation of sound, used by musicians, speech analysts and countless others) or ultrasonics (a common use being the imaging of a foetus during pregnancy).

One relatively new field of acoustics, called archaeoacoustics, aims to determine certain physical properties of caves and other natural geological formations by gauging precisely how they respond to sound sources. A fascinating splinter application of archaeoacoustics has been dubbed 'human echolocation', whereby a person cultivates an ability to deduce the properties of ancient sites by emitting whistles or humming noises and gauging precisely how these change in relation to the acoustic properties of the space itself. Echolocation has irresistible connotations with prehistoric ritualistic practices, the evidence of which can readily be found painted on the walls of caves such as in Lascaux, southern France. It has even been proposed that these correlate with gateways to spiritual awakening and specific belief systems, though our understanding of such philosophies and practices is limited.

Among other interesting branches of acoustics, we have aeroacoustics, which besides helping designers of wind and brass instruments such as flutes and trumpets, can be applied to the field of noise limitation for aircraft in regard to turbulence. Related to this area of acoustics is active noise control in headphones and the design and refinement of hearing aids.

It's reassuring to know that the human ear is still the most valuable means of filtering meaningful sound from the less meaningful. We are still further from understanding the limits to human imagination and comprehension when it comes to sound than we are from being able to quantify, identify and filter its components. The beauty of a sound surely has at least as much to do with human perception as reception; in other words, it is what, why and how our brains process sounds which determines their impact for us, not merely their amplitude, frequency or timbre as discerned by machines. Everyday sounds, just as with music, defy adequate description or evaluation within the emotional spectrum. Besides, for each of us, this emotional spectrum is likely to be made up of different elements.

If you and I hear the same sound and deduce it to be a door bell ringing, how can we know we are hearing it the same way, let alone deriving similar meaning from it? For you, the door bell might resemble a xylophone you once played at school, while for me the sound

The beauty of a sound has as much to do with perception as reception

might instantly remind me of the entrance to my grandmother's nursing home. In each case, the sound, the environment in which we hear it and its immediate connotations cannot be disentangled: the sound and its emotional/historical/contextual meanings all roll into one. The ever-widening field of

acoustics continues to increase our appreciation and awareness of sound, but thankfully we don't need machines to decode, let alone *interpret* sound for us; we already have our ears, our imagination and our diverse perspectives of life to help us do this perfectly well.

Psychoacoustics

Whereas musical acoustics is primarily concerned with how instruments make their sound, psychoacoustics ventures into a vast hinterland of more speculative areas, such as the relationship between acoustics and cognition, or between biological sound and human perception. What the mind 'does' with a sound when different levels of auditory stimuli are fed to it, is an aspect of cognitive neuroscience which has attracted a multitude of ingenious approaches. At a perhaps more obvious level, our receptivity to fast, repetitive music, such as dance, hip-hop or even certain jazz and classical forms, seems to result in a physical reaction to the faster brain waves triggered by it; the converse appears to be true of slower, less repetitive forms also.

By extension, physical responses measurable in the central nervous system can be understood to correlate broadly with the type of sound experienced. It would seem reasonable to propose that non-musical sounds possessing a range of intensities and volumes might trigger a similar range of physical and emotional responses in us.

A further offshoot from the idea of sound stimulating a physical response has come from analysing adults' reaction times to the sound of a baby crying. A recent study proposed that listening to a baby crying over a prolonged period (five minutes) increased both the decisiveness and speed of response of forty adults. It is thought that we may be hard-wired to respond to this sound as a call to action, a suggestion backed up by the fact that in the same study, participants reacted less immediately and assertively to the sound of high-pitched bird songs, or to women crying. [Source: Professor Morten Kringelbach of MindLab, posted on sciencenordic. com]. It is further suggested that undergoing exercises of this nature might improve our reactions in a more general sense, and that most baby animals have a range of noises that have evolved to capture their parents' attention.

The Diagnostic Potential of Biomusic

Using sounds such as birdsong, animal noises, those derived from plants or as in this case, the human body, experiments with biomusic began in the 1920s and interest continues to grow. Long considered to be conducive to mindful practice, an intriguing article from 2016 entitled 'Biomusic: An auditory interface for detecting physiological indicators in children' (Cheung, Han Kushki, Anagnostou and Biddiss), showed that biomusic can also facilitate the detection of anxiety in children whose capacity for verbal/gestural communication is

impaired. Electrodermal activity (the electrical conductivity of skin, affected by changes to emotional response) is mapped to melody, skin temperature to musical key, heart rate to a drum beat and respiration to a so-called 'whooshing' sound akin to breath exhalation. By comparing the recorded bio--music generated by these three discrete processes, a kind of sound algorithm results for each emotional state: 'anxious' or 'relaxed'. Biomusic from a small number of 'typically' developing children was compared alongside those with autism spectrum disorders, across a range of calm and anxiety-induced conditions. It was provisionally concluded that non-specialist caregivers can use this as valuable feedback and tailor their response more quickly and optimally. Such experiments are of course subject to a variety of potentially problematic aspects, not least being that, by definition, the individuals being evaluated are not able to confirm its validity or otherwise. Nonetheless, the potential to use biomusic as a diagnostic tool is an exciting one.

Artificial Intelligence

When we stop to think of what we expect our brain to do in an instant, perhaps distinguishing between a matrix of voices (with a variety of accents and paces of delivery), music and other sounds all cutting across each other, we should marvel at the current gulf between human intelligence and artificial intelligence (AI). AI can go some way to mimicking human

skills and perceptions via algorithms and so-called 'machine learning'. And in recent times, AI has been used promisingly in the medium of sound art and sound design, whereby analysable aspects of multiple pieces of music, voices and noises become fused together and extrapolated from to produce entirely new pieces of music.

These systems have already begun to find their way into the creation of meditation tracks, and other potentially valuable ways of bringing us closer to our inner selves may be just around the corner. One can imagine how, in the future, an individual's highly

We can rely on nature's majestically random algorithms

specific needs might be better met by AI, so that we can dial up the sounds we need on demand, whether for a meditation or other purpose. Until that time, we must rely on the majestically random algorithms from nature.

A part of me wonders whether supply already risks exceeding demand when it comes to AI – could we be throwing valuable resources at mimicking those things which we already have at our disposal, when we'd be better off learning even more about our own minds, perceptions and behaviours? On the other hand, we can never accurately predict which uses technological and intellectual advances will ultimately be best put to, and in the meantime, we may as well see how far we can push the boundaries.

CHAPTER TWO

PATHWAYS TO SOUND

Zen Buddhism reminds us to invest more in meditation, inner reflection and intuition, rather than to try to fathom the unfathomable. Coming to terms with the things we cannot change frees up space in our lives to contemplate the things we can change. The purpose of Zen isn't literally to silence the mind — not that we'd be able to sustain this for long in any case — but to accept non-judgementally the waves of thought which trickle in and out of our minds as if they'd come from someone or somewhere else.

THE POINT OF SOUND

◆

Until we've noticed it, all sound is a mere possibility. The sound doesn't mind if it goes unnoticed or not; the question is, are we ready to gain something from it? If so, why not embrace it straight away, let it wash over us until we're ready to pass it on to someone else?

THERE'S ALWAYS THE CHANCE that having reverberated its way through our mind, sound will have altered ever so slightly, become filtered by whatever thoughts had been lingering. Its point of departing is, just like our grip on the present moment, a point of our choosing.

Imagine twenty people in a room, all silently listening to someone speaking – now imagine 200 people, or 2,000. The voice itself, the starting point of the sounding event, is exactly the same, and yet it can still only be as valuable as the point of its reception; an audience of one is exactly the same as an audience of a thousand, since there is no such thing as collective listening. But when shared, the words spoken by the voice may well seem even more precious and immutable.

Bottled Blissfulness

If we could bottle blissfulness, it would doubtless be immediately available from every high street kiosk, probably with organic options, packaged biodegradably, retro-style. Some of us would sip it; others would glug the lot in a single hit. But

perhaps bottled blissfulness would lose its potency over time, become just another overpriced commodity, or a black market might rise up, bottling counterfeit blissfulness, and subvert the very point of it.

Soon we'd take blissfulness for granted. We'd begin to feel tense the moment we realize our blissfulness bottle is half empty, so we'd stock up in advance, no matter who else may be missing out. In the end, once our stock of blissfulness has begun to run dry, we would realize that it is easily squandered or taken for granted, and that blissfulness only endures when we have other people with whom to share it and help us nurture it. Blissfulness, it might eventually occur to us, is better not bottled, but left unhurriedly trickling through precious minerals in some deep imaginary cave; for it's the moving towards it at a time and pace of our own choosing, or conversely its very randomness, that makes its discovery worth the wait. Perhaps, in the end, we'd start looking for ways to encourage others around us to sip more sparingly from the blissfulness goblet, and cherish those moments where we have been able to gift a little of it to someone else, preferably at our own expense.

We are none of us entitled to feel blissfulness. It will often come at a price to the rest of us. Besides, knowing how fleeting a moment of it is might encourage us to be more attentive to it when it appears, out of the blue. In this Anthropocene epoch, where we are at last acknowledging what humans are contributing to the Great Acceleration – an unprecedented era of lost empathy for our planet – the idea of blissfulness and entitlement is the very antipathy to accepting global culpability.

Sound as Commodity

The staggering rise in popularity of online music videos suggests we are slowly turning into a generation that *watches* music. Meanwhile, advertisements have become a quasi-art form in themselves – we could sit in a cinema watching what we think is the opening scene to a movie, only to realize a minute later that we've been duped into admiring an advert for car insurance. In this ever-expanding pleasure-bubble, consumer, voyeur and protagonist have become barely distinguishable from each other as video games, virtual reality, animation and fantasy steadily blur into one. This could hardly contrast more vividly with what happens in our brains when we read a good novel: the casting, cinematography and sound-sculpting miraculously come together in the cutting room of our own imagination.

At a grass roots level, a burgeoning industry of soundtrack creators and self-styled laptop musicians now fulfil a role unimaginable to the pencil-wielding film score composer of yesteryear. But the artful blending of stock sound effects, live and computer-generated music, pre-engineered sounds and post-production editing hasn't necessarily led to a rise in quality, only quantity or immediacy. Our response to this multimedia superabundance is beginning to feel more and more scripted, too: there is a danger that we are becoming swayed more by the tech-packaging than by the worthiness, sincerity or morality of the message. We press a button on our handheld device and expect some kind of noise or haptic reaction – an acknowledgement that we are functioning as others

---

MINDFULNESS EXERCISE

BLISSFUL SOUNDS

One way we might inch closer to the apocryphal blissfulness bottle is to discover those sounds that help us to *feel* it. Blissful sounds don't have a universal currency; bliss can be an emotion felt as we sit silently alone in a pine forest, or packed into a football stadium among thousands of fellow spectators; it might simply be in the company of our family, eating birthday cake. A blissful sound isn't one we'll all find together in a moment of mass enlightenment, it's something we must all search out and hold dear for ourselves. Make a point of connecting to a sound that has true meaning for you – don't gorge on it, or it may start to sound less special; but know where it is, and access it when the moment feels right. Perhaps you have a church or temple on your walk home from work, where a certain sound and ambience always reaches out to you, or an old bicycle shop that plays the music you adored as a teenager. Add these to your bank of blissful sound environments, then go ahead and treat yourself. This is the low-hanging fruit, your most easily accessible sound library.

do. The beeps and squelches that punctuate our insecurities have become a predatory menace.

It seems inevitable we must all to some extent succumb to the commoditizing not just of visual media, but *sound*; and yet this threatens to diminish our capacity to engage with natural sound at the simplest, most direct and beneficial level. When sound is supplied even when it is not demanded, we become progressively numb to the possibility of the spontaneous pearl-like elaborations of a fish breaking the surface of its watery home or a whistling cab driver. Availability quickly tips into superabundance, which leads to casual expectation. There is no reason to suppose we cannot enjoy both – the advantages of HD-streamed digital entertainment and the primordial music of a tree swaying to the waltz of an evening breeze – but this will require us to be more mindful of what we subject our ears to.

ASMR

ASMR, or autonomous sensory meridian response, has steadily been gaining traction across the internet, most recently in gaming. ASMR is an attempt to explain the physical tingling sensations experienced in direct response to certain stimuli, typically videos or audio. This can be especially effective in conjunction with the human voice when delivered in a soft, slow manner. In ASMR we can experience something akin to the effect gained when in intimate physical

MINDFULNESS EXERCISE

TAKE A RETREAT FROM NOISY NOTIFICATIONS

Apart from perhaps your phone's ringtone, do you really need all those customized sound notifications? What would happen if you turned them off – and perhaps your social media popup messages while you're about it? You might recover a little headspace, and into the bargain you could find you are noticing more than you did. Your devices easily become the time-and-motion advocates of your day, notifying you of things that you don't really need to be notified about, like your plumber's birthday or the bread maker your cat-sitter's currently considering buying. All those impudent interruptions fatigue your mind and weigh heavily on your sense of guilt – will my plumber be offended if I don't send him birthday wishes? Perhaps I should warn the cat-sitter against buying that particular brand of bread maker? Notifications have a tendency to pester and distract us from what we would otherwise regard as important. Notifications – especially sound notifications – are mostly a self-serving scourge; we don't need them, *they need us* – ignore them, they're just attention-seeking.

Your first day with the sound turned off will probably feel disconcerting – have people forgotten to interact with me? Perhaps I'm missing out on something hilarious? The truth is that you run a far greater risk of missing out on real life happening right under your nose. Give your ears a treat and snuff out the affliction of sound notifications. Within no time you'll find you are glancing at your phone less often and not feeling burdened by other people's trivialities. Let that bumblebee heading for your lavender bush be the kind of sound notification worthy of your undivided attention.

contact with others. Examples of this could include massage, nail-painting or beard-trimming. Animals in the wild can spend a considerable amount of time grooming each other, and this is widely accepted to be more than mutual hygiene. Though the term ASMR was apparently coined around a decade ago, the underlying concept would be harder to pin down to any one person or moment in time. Oblique references have been traced at least as far back as a century ago in the novels of Virginia Woolf, though we might stumble over examples of ASMR-like sensations in much older forms of literature, art, drama or music.

Some types of reaction – described as 'brain massage' or AIHO (attention induced head orgasm) – can come in response to ambient noises. People experiencing ASMR report sensing a tingle that typically begins in the scalp, neck or upper body. In extremely sensitive people these sensations could shimmer down through the entire body. We might have a positive ASMR reaction to hearing certain sounds that arise naturally from the world around us. These could include a woodpecker busily at work in a forest, or a waterfall roaring magnificently in the distance. An infinite number of human-made sounds are capable of triggering something not dissimilar, such as sand gushing from the back of a builder's lorry, or the clonk of old books being carefully replaced onto shelves in a library.

An adverse reaction could come from the sound of finger-nails scratching on a blackboard, noisy eating or the music

coming from someone else's earphones, though we won't all necessarily agree where a positive tingle morphs into a negative shudder. Fingers tapping on a table is another human sound that reportedly provokes a decisive ASMR reaction.

It would appear from the many examples available on the internet that humans can stimulate these kinds of reactions with remarkable ease. A so-called 'ASMRtist' is a person attempting to bring about such reactions in a controlled way, typically through video. Often the effect will be heightened by means of a soothing voice chosen to reinforce the tranquil mood. Perhaps unsurprisingly, the combination of an atmospheric pastoral scene and a poetically slow, reflective vocal tone works especially well in product advertising. We're all familiar with adverts depicting a popping of champagne corks in the foyer of a swanky hotel, or expensive perfume being unwrapped in a chauffeur-driven limousine.

On balance, it would be cynical to suggest that ASMR has become just another way of coaxing money from the unwary, or the latest fad to fuel online media manipulation. Besides, a video, art installation or piece of music could be deemed effective as an ASMR trigger even though it may have been conceived for an entirely different purpose decades or even centuries earlier. Media has a long history of being repurposed in such ways – for example, online videos showing viewers how to apply make-up have later been found to have persuasive ASMR qualities.

RECORD YOUR OWN MEDITATION SOUNDTRACK

There are plenty of downloadable soundtracks for meditation, some complete with wind chimes, whale noises or other potentially conducive bolt-ons, but recording your own meditation soundtrack couldn't be easier. Just whip out your phone or tablet, place it strategically (somewhere only ambient sounds will be picked up) and you're good to go. Place it on a soft surface where vibrations are minimized, perhaps at an oblique angle if in a room. Simply let your device capture what it will over as long as you feel inclined, and once you've stocked up a few, you'll know what works best for you. Twenty minutes is ideal for me.

Record a few in a woodland setting or your garden, others in a café or similar environment, away from too much clatter and chatter – a beach, or even a cliff top could be good too, though handheld recording devices don't take kindly to gusts of wind, rumbling or extremes of pitch. Your recordings don't need to be made at a high resolution, so you should be able to store up quite a few. A friend of mine enjoys recording himself walking; the sound of his trudging adds a frisson of personal involvement. If there is a sound you find aids your meditation, let it dominate a little more. Keep in mind the purpose of your recording is to meditate, so avoid scenarios where sudden intrusive noises seem likely, or where there is the distinct possibility of people talking loudly.

Making your own soundtrack is itself a mindful task. Don't miss the opportunity to meditate as you harvest your sound, beginning only when you feel free of other distractions. Slowly invite the sounds to pour across your conscious and subconscious as you gradually move your mind away from practicalities and trivialities.

There will be those who feel there is an emperor's new clothes dimension to ASMR, or that it capitalizes on our ever-curious thirst for new ways of stating the obvious. Clearly this is not the prevailing view among those who gain something from it, so until you have tried ASMR for yourself, it might be safer to keep an open mind. Research suggests that a significant percentage of the population have no capacity to experience these tingling sensations, or at least not in direct response to the kind of stimuli mentioned here, and yet it might be interesting to have sight of a rather larger, more empirical basis for evaluating ASMR than the data currently to hand. Oddly perhaps, despite an unquestionably rising interest in ASMR, many of us appear to have little or no direct experience of it. Who knows, ASMR might turn out to be the most helpful stimulus for meditation you've never heard of?

An Arctic Voyage

I once gave concerts on a small cruise ship which wended its way north from Bergen, Norway, to Isfjord, Spitsbergen, one of the world's most remote dwelling places; for a few months of the year the small island is plunged into darkness. This phenomenon would be very strange for most of us, and yet is quite normal for residents of this curiously beautiful place.

One day, the captain announced he would turn off the engines and we would drift in silence for a short while. It was one of those magical moments I'll never forget – a teal sky,

biscuit-crisp ice stretching out as far as the eye could see, the air as sharp and thin as a razor. An eerie silence seemed to enshroud us; I closed my eyes and listened to the ice cracking arrhythmically in this strange light, a noise defying description, but perhaps lying somewhere between a whisper and the final crackles of a dying fire.

During the thirty minutes I stood there, transfixed, the temperature seemed to plummet a few further degrees. An occasional stoical character meandered tentatively around the deck wrapped in blankets, taking photos and pointing out the slightest sign of movement from beneath the icy surface.

For me, the experience was one of my senses oddly coming together as one – I was tasting the cold, smelling the cutting breeze, feeling the sound of the cracking ice in my bones and hearing my breath respond to the ever-changing light. What better spot to feel freed from the strictures of time, where seconds and minutes seem to clump together in slow motion, rather like the ice formations themselves. It felt as though time itself had been placed on pause, not just our little ship, temporarily marooned in this perilously majestic place, far from any realistic rescue aid.

A sensory experience such as this can make us lose our orientation and make meditation almost irresistible and inevitable. Try pausing on a moonlit walk, and allow your senses to combine as you immerse yourself in the moment, hearing, tasting, smelling and feeling your surroundings.

SOUND AND EMOTION

Using words to describe an emotion, or indeed a sound, is as flimsy as the emotion or sound itself; and the sentences we formulate unthinkingly are like birds which could fly off in any direction at the whim of the moment.

THE BRAIN IS EXTRAORDINARILY EFFECTIVE at turning sound into emotion. Neuroscientists, psychologists and philosophers can propose reasons for some of these preternatural transformations, but by no means is it possible to logic away all of what they suspect is occurring. Attempts at explaining such associations are in any case constrained by the limitations of words themselves: our verbal outpourings are not scripted, but are infinitely adaptable – we might know the essence of what we wish to convey as we begin a sentence, but then it'll change; a single thought deviation, interruption or environmental distraction could launch us into an entirely different direction and land us in no-man's-land.

The area of the brain which stores auditory information is the auditory dorsal stream; in particular the premotor and prefrontal regions, which deal with motor sequence information – not just how we tuck away a melody, but also the patterning of non-musical sounds. The extent to which this storing process embraces spoken (or perhaps even imagined) language and syntax – the rhythmic proportioning and

assembly of words to construct meaning – is not known. Clearly, poets, rappers and others whose currency is words connected in lengthy, complex chains must also be storing these away with every bit as much efficiency as a violinist who can summon a dozen concertos at the drop of a hat.

Sound Association

It appears that we often associate a particular sound with an experience lodged inside us. For me, an ambulance siren occasionally stirs up the memory of a motorcycle accident I witnessed in my teens, and the vulture-like screech of a masonry drill invariably conjures up comforting memories of my father perpetually fixing something in the house when I was a child. But perhaps for you a similar drilling sound drags up the memory of a painful trip to the dentist. The sound may be the same, but its emotional journey deep into the auditory cortex will be as unique as the brain in the head of the person who hears it. I'm partly convinced these little bobbins of sound-information, individually wrapped in emotional value, are the brain's way of storing important memories.

I can also imagine that the converse might be true, too – that an emotion might trigger in us a specific sound – or perhaps, even more fancifully, cause us to *imagine* such a sound just before we make it. When we verbalize a memory, we unwittingly endow it with a particular range of tone colours, so that those who know us unquestioningly pick up

'The tongue can paint what the eye can't see.'

CHINESE PROVERB

its authenticity. We've all evolved a subtle repertoire of sighs and vocalizations; these personalized prefixes, suffixes, sniffs and culturally skewed variants on 'ums' and 'ahs' convey as much meaning as the words themselves. And when it comes to our lexicon of pauses and changes of pitch, spontaneous inflections or more calculated emphases, our spoken language takes on a whole galaxy of potential meanings.

A skilled musician or actor is practised at repurposing the bond between sound and emotion. In their own ways, they persuade us that their characterizations are unambiguous and meaningful. More strategically, on the other hand, a politician may attempt to trap us in the lair of an emotive statement delivered in a tone designed to distract us from its shallowness (or untruthfulness). These are examples of sound-emotion used in what could be described as manipulative ways, or at the very least fashioned to solicit a particular response, though I'm of course not suggesting such exhortations are necessarily devoid of sincerity. Who among us can dissociate Martin Luther King's 'I have a dream' speech from the intense quiver in his voice? The emotional message is inextricably linked to the words and the tone used to convey them; these words are like rivers flowing from an ocean of inner meaning. When we

read a book, we construct a voice and style of delivery for each character, and who knows whether these are based on hybrids of familiar personalities or new, derived entirely from the clues we pick up from the page? Fantasy and reality blur so easily for us that sound, emotion, meaning and hallucination frequently spill over into each other.

Though our tone will almost invariably betray something of our emotion, we cannot presume we are able to gauge accurately the reactions in those who happen to be listening. When we exchange emotions via the imperfect medium of verbal language,

The power of sound to mould emotion is infinitely impressive

we expect an amount of it to miss its mark, an obvious example being when we speak over the phone, since there are no visual markers to help us decode inevitable ambiguities, sarcasm, double-entendres or attempts at self-effacement. A blind person, on the other hand, must rely solely upon sound as a conduit to the emotion that triggered it, and I cannot help supposing their intuitive ability to fathom meaning is as a result better than for the rest of us. Since we might adduce a hundred meanings from a single pair of commonly used words, purely because of these sound-based variables, the idea that our brain is like memory foam does not square. Or if it is, then the power of sound to shape and mould emotion is infinitely more impressive than we could ever imagine.

Learn from your Mindful Cat

We cannot presume knowledge of a cat's thinking or under-standing – for all we know, it's not chasing that rabbit for fun, or even for food, but in response to a higher-level cat-voice instructing it to rid the world of floppy-eared Leporidae mammals. At the risk of humanizing our pets, let's assume for a moment that a cat is simply what we imagine it to be, insa-tiable in its quest for tranquillity and warmth, suspicious only of other cats that venture onto its patch, never doubtful of its owner's love, always happy to consider the prospect of a meal, eternally grateful for a moment's affection.

For me, it's the sound my cat Ethel makes, which I'm con-vinced is always tailored to match my mood, that I find to be most mindful, meditative and restorative. She's not speaking to me, as such, and yet somehow I feel communicated to, through her range of affectionate and appreciative purrs. Every cat has its own vocabulary of sounds for snoozing and cleaning, its own timbres, which we associate with its antici-pation of affection or food. We also instantly recognize when trouble is afoot, or when the moment for spider hunting has won over lap time. Each of these sounds is as personal and special to its owner as the chuckle their closest friend makes.

In truth, my cat is probably more mindful than I am, more content to savour the moment, not ambitious for anything more than it is receiving from me right now. I am confident that my cat will never question my ulterior motives for tick-

ling its neck. Simply sitting for half an hour with a cat on your lap is a curious form of therapy; by relating to how your cat feels about you, you learn to accept this is being reciprocated, and this cycle of unconditional caring builds your ability to experience self-compassion as well as compassion for others. If there is a sound to unconditional love, for me it's the sound Ethel makes when she suddenly notices I'm there.

Our tendency towards ruminative thought, for troubling over the what-ifs of life, is the price we pay for our impressive intelligence and elementally cast cognitive powers. We take for granted that we can outsmart an animal through our powers of reasoning and evaluation, but this comes at the cost of a mind rarely at peace with itself. Unlike our cat, we find it harder to take human relationships at face value and are instead prone to cynicism, perhaps in some primeval bid to self-protect or head off negative potential. Instead of helping us to fathom the answers to life's more challenging questions, our looping high-octane brain frequently serves to incapacitate us, to take us further away from resolutions to issues we can actually live with. I somehow doubt that a cat craves after our intellectual powers, our ability to engineer a bridge or compose a symphony, and yet I'm more confident there are times we would swap places with our cat, if only when we witness its ability to shrug off unfairness within seconds of experiencing it.

MINDFULNESS EXERCISE

A PENNY FOR YOUR THOUGHTS

The sound a small coin makes when it lands on a stone floor immediately alerts the ear and sets the imagination in a spin. Like a tiny revolving cymbal, or a scaled-down figure skater, it commands our attention, however inconspicuous its fall from your pocket. There are a million ways its miniature dance might end — an elegant curtsy perhaps, or more energetically, like a hummingbird poised for its sugary nectar feast.

Record a coin spinning, preferably in a reverberant corridor or walled courtyard where its shimmer will appear to last a little longer. See how quietly you can employ it as a ringtone on your phone, or use it to trigger a brief meditation. Once you've learned to associate a spell of tranquillity with its mesmerizing silvery timbre, you'll use it to slip easily into a treasured personal space somewhere deep inside you. The sound of a penny, dime or cent magicked into life has a currency beyond its face value; keep it precious.

CHAPTER THREE

MEDITATION SOUNDED OUT

A poet's or opera composer's vision of humanity's place in the material world is allowed to be unsettled, questioning, in turmoil and under siege. But in mindfulness we have the opposite goal of course, to feel illuminated and inspired by life, enchanted by the opportunities it may throw at us, at peace with who we already are and not distracted by energy-sapping self-doubt. We are not trying to claim moral high ground, but to level ourselves.

SATIPATTHANA

There are so many forms of meditation — perhaps hundreds. Every one of the growing number of books in this series offers a practical, real-world illustration of how these forms of meditation can be channelled or utilized in pursuit of a mind better at ease with itself and its own emotions.

ONE OF THE BEST-KNOWN FORMS is 'transcendental meditation' (The Beatles got heavily into this in the late 1960s), whereby repeating a mantra or other sound over and over again helps us to transcend the things we glibly lump together as 'thoughts'. But it surely isn't such a stretch to trade a repeated word for a repeated *action*, whether it's kneading dough, striking a squash ball up and down a wall — or even washing dishes?

'Dynamic meditation' is a considerably more energetic form of meditation than most — practitioners of dynamic meditation might resemble people dancing wildly; the goal here is to dynamically force out previously ingrained thought patterns and simultaneously replace these with more helpful ones. It would be hard to sum up the myriad forms of 'religious meditation' in under a few thousand pages, suffice it to say that virtually every religion can lay claim to its own bespoke version, or versions; often, but by no means exclusively, these will be centred on acts of tranquillity, inward

reflection, scripture or prayer. Drawing from a close exami-
nation of such rituals, the early Hindu religion (roughly 500
years BCE) became of interest to the Buddha, who stream-
lined and repurposed these old traditions into what would
become known as *Satipatthana* – the form of meditation closest to what we know as 'mindfulness meditation'.

The word 'Satipatthana' is wonderfully rhythmic – you
could even turn it into a mantra; it just trips off the tongue –
say it to yourself a few times, quietly and thoughtfully,
throwing the emphasis to the
fourth of its five syllables:
Sa-ti-pat-*tha*-na'. Actually, the
word splits down conveniently
into three parts: *sati* (meaning
'attention'), *upa* (meaning 'inside') and *thana* (meaning 'to
keep'). The goal is unambiguous and neatly holistic – *to keep
your attention inside*. Satipatthana is the wilful counterpart to
the so-called 'monkey mind', the tendency most of us have to
allow our thoughts to tumble over each other chaotically, like
the unruly primates we descended from. As we learn to notice
our own reactions to life's challenges and conundrums, we
can teach ourselves to repurpose the less promising ones and
thereby make allies with them. This logic is deceptively tricky,
but well worth trying to incorporate: when there is a noise –
either literally or metaphorically – beckon it *into* your mind,
embrace it, befriend it and sense it losing its control over you.

Virtually every religion has its own form of meditation

Quietude and Disquietude

The pursuit of mindfulness chimes well with the idea that we are attempting to transition from disquietude to quietude — from a state of anxiety or unease to one of calmness and serenity. In turn, serenity implies or yearns for silence. Poets, storytellers, writers and musicians make frequent use of the notion of disquietude; the arts have always used tension and release, ebb and flow, light and shade. There will be those who insist that we cannot experience serenity without also experiencing its opposite force — anxiety. The younger generation has been pessimistically described as Generation Anxious, and it may be correct to say that our world now has greater potential for children to feel at odds with what it should ideally mean to be young and free. Children deserve to live in a calmer world than the one we currently force them to navigate, and inspirational young people, such as Greta Thunberg,

---

'Here had lived an elder race, to which we look back with disquietude. The country which we visit at week-ends was really a home to it, and the graver sides of life, the deaths, the partings, the yearnings for love, have their deepest expression in the heart of the fields.'

FROM 'HOWARDS END' BY E.M. FORSTER,
EDWARD ARNOLD, LONDON, 1910

are leading the way by taking decisive action to address these challenges. If we could pass on serenity and mindfulness to our young people, what an achievement that would be. Finding inner quiet is the key to making disquiet disappear.

The Sound of a Sleeping Moth

When we think of how a moth seems attracted to a light bulb, and how feverishly its wings are working, it makes me wonder what, beyond confusion, a moth is feeling or hearing. Contrary to popular opinion, moths are not really attracted to unnatural light. Rather, they are struggling desperately to recalibrate their navigational equipment, which has been thrown off kilter by what they thought was the moon: a form of fatal attraction.

If moths lived in a lightless world, would they head for the moon in torrents, like rain in reverse? And if we lived in a world where sound had never existed, presumably we would have evolved some sixth sense to compensate?

Only some moths have 'ears', and these are membranes that are situated in the thorax, though the greater wax moth has evolved minutely sensitive tympanal membranes with which it can detect predatory bats. Presumably other moths have not evolved ear-like appendages because they simply don't need them, and yet surely most living creatures, however large or small, utilize vibrations in some form or other, either as a means of communication, measuring distance,

gauging the weather, assessing danger levels or searching for food or a mate. There seems to be an endless bounty of moths – I counted eight varieties in my bathroom last week, most seemingly in a state of repose, or what I permit myself to imagine is quiet contemplation. I can't know what a moth is thinking, or even whether thinking is an appropriate word to describe the feelings or primeval responses it might be capable of experiencing during its brief life; whether it has the capacity to dream as we do, know its place in the world, hanker after something beyond realistic grasp, or regret an opportunity missed.

For all I know, your average moth is an athlete of the mind, perceiving beyond its diminutive form the riddles and contradictions of its zoomed-in natural world. But let us suppose for a moment that a moth is doing all of these things; noticing, taking in sound, contemplating a spectrum of meanings and enjoying being a part, however inconceivably small, of its surroundings. That moth, silhouetted magnificently on the wall, may actually be sizing us up, just as we do it, wondering what purpose our perpetual thundering around could possibly have. I want to imagine that a moth enters its meditative state so utterly and unquestioningly that its stressful moments are as rare as our moments of true serenity. And maybe, to take this fantasy further, as it sleeps it has memories of the day – or better still, imagined memories of its previous lives as a chrysalis or caterpillar.

I wonder what we can learn from a moth, a creature that may only live for a week or two; or what we can picture it thinking as it assumes its improbable temporary home on the edge of a window latch. The sound of a sleeping moth may as well be what we hope it is, just as the moth has my permission to imagine whatever it wants about what I'm hearing as I sleep. A year in the life of a brown house moth will be its only year, and perhaps just one third of this time will be spent as an adult. Its time in the larval and pupal stages soaks up two-thirds or more of its entire life cycle; perhaps this surreal state of expectant suspension is meaningful to the moth itself as it finally shrugs off its long gestation and spreads its wings for the very first time. We may be tempted to pity a moth's short life, but for all we know it could be one of supreme, unfettered beauty and tranquillity, the like of which no Buddhist can ever aspire to. Perhaps a moth's sense of what it is reflects the telescoped timeframe of its animated existence; after all, its every passing day is equivalent to a full year for us.

The Sanctuary of Silence

We often speak of silence as being uncomfortable or unsettling: 'you could cut the silence with a knife', 'an awkward silence befell the room', or 'he suffered in silence'. But this is surely only because we have lost the capacity to savour silence for the value it holds, and also perhaps because we have grown used to associating silence with an *absence* of something, an

embarrassing noise vacuum, rather than being a valuable 'thing'. Logically, peace of mind will come so much more easily from *peace* itself, since this is the state that gives it the freedom to be. In silence we cannot gauge the passing of time – not if we have truly relaxed our grip on thought – since it is thought that keeps that damned clock ticking. Maybe we should stop trying to 'capture' a moment's silence and just recognize it to be there, patiently waiting for our *inattention*.

We punish the worst criminals with periods of solitary confinement – enforced silence and solitude – but surely this is an indictment of our incapacity to frame silence and achieve self-containment in a positive, productive way? After all, for a person compelled to live near a motorcycle racetrack, silence could be the best tonic imaginable. Silence is something that captains of industry are slowly waking up to, by encouraging their workforce to sit in silence for just a couple of minutes each day. Silence apparently increases productivity, as well as mental and physical health, and has even been shown to help generate new brain cells.

The sound of true silence is something we can only imagine; it's impossible for us to truly experience silence because even in an anechoic (soundproofed) chamber we will hear our body going about its chores, pumping blood and oxygen around, digesting food, and so on. But surely this ought not to stop us from aspiring to the possibility of silence? A good start is to get yourself some noise-cancelling headphones and lie

down in a neutral place; I find lying on the floor strangely conducive to my near-silence experience, perhaps because it brings me that little bit more in touch with terra firma.

The Man on the Moon

From here I sometimes picture I'm on the moon, ambling weightlessly and noiselessly along the Sea of Tranquillity. It's not a real sea, in any case, though for the longest period astronomers thought those dark shadowy smudges we can see with the naked eye might be the equivalent to the Earth's deepest oceans. If I can allow myself to imagine the impossibility of silence, then meandering aimlessly on the moon surely isn't such a stretch? Better still, I can picture this apocryphal sea instantly transformed into a soundless, tide-less, boundless abyss, surrounded by toothy rocks positioned conveniently as places to savour a moment's repose. I might even allow myself to admire a dreamed-up sun reflecting its purple light up into the cliff tops grimacing down at me pityingly from an improbable height. This music of silence is as unending as it is unbeginning, and as easy on the ear as Mozart or any caramel-toned blues singer. As I wend my way unhurriedly through this chicaning moonscape I might occasionally turn my head back in the direction of Earth, not in some absent-minded bid to trace out the Great Wall of China with my fingernail, but to see if I can remember what noise sounds like. If we have ears it is to entertain the possibility of sound,

whether wanted or unwanted, and yet noise is usually the reason I'd be happy to don my astronaut's helmet and vacate a little head space, if only for five minutes. I can almost feel the tug of the Earth's magnetic field sucking me back into its orbit as I hold my breath in awe of this majestic, undulating mass of collided meteorites and comets. There's no cow flying over my moon, but I wouldn't turn a hair even if there were; I might even draw its shape in the seabed with my toe. Luckily my resolve is as firm as any earthly magnetic attraction; besides, my grip on these imagined rocks is every bit as strong as my brief state of unreality.

Find your own silence, or better still, create a little for yourself. I've left a bit of the moon free for your own use, should you feel like joining me up there. Alternatively, you might discover a few seconds of silence peeping out from under a rock at the bottom of your garden, or whispering at you from your sock drawer. You don't need to have been brought up by wolves to appreciate the many shades of near

---

'See how nature – trees, flowers, grass –
grows in silence; see the stars, the moon and the sun,
how they move in silence. . . We need silence to
be able to touch souls.'
MOTHER TERESA OF CALCUTTA (1910–1997)

silence you can draw towards you in your meditations, or to count your blessings when you at last discover your very own sanctuary of silence. Silence may be theoretically impossible for us, but only if we insist on acknowledging reality; everywhere else, silence seems as commonplace as sand on a beach or the house-sized blocks of cheese stacked up on my side of the moon.

There is a knack to silence. A person accomplished in it probably becomes a better listener, and certainly a person used to economizing with words when needed. If you were told you had to take a fully silent retreat for one quarter of every month, as in a Zen monastery, you'd become satisfied with less by way of outside stimuli, relate more easily to the needs and habits of others, and learn to flush out those thoughts which are not contributing positively to your life. You'd tune in to the patterns of nature more readily – you'd notice more how the wind and rain sound different as each season turns, and the precise point in the year when certain birds appear to be more active or less energetic. The aspects of physical sensation you might currently take for granted, such as the existence of your body, would invite a different kind of interrogation, so that through silence a new presence would be awarded to each limb, each individual part of your body.

When we cut down on noise – even by a few minutes each day – we enjoy all the more the time when we are experiencing sound. When we take the time to be silent and observe

MINDFULNESS EXERCISE

HOLD THAT THOUGHT

Begin by finding somewhere away from obvious distractions. If possible, make it into a simple space, one without stuff cluttering it. It doesn't need to resemble a monastery, library or sun-drenched field with nodding sunflowers; it could even be on a bus. If you live in a noisy household, you could try imposing a two-minute noise embargo; it can be surprising just how addicted to sound you, your colleagues or family members have become – people sit in a room and immediately *have* to have some kind of noise for company; or else they *have* to pick up their phone and begin scrolling. Next, practise the vital skill of accepting an instruction from yourself: 'I'm going to be silent for one whole minute'. Keep your eyes open if you prefer, or close them if the visual noise of your surroundings has for whatever reason become overly invasive.

At first, keeping silent is your only goal, not what happens next. For many people, even this initial task will be difficult. Build up gradually to two minutes, then three, and notice how you are slowly able to sharpen your decision to be inactive to a point where time stands still, just as you sit still. Keep in mind that the object is not to find more time for yourself – you have not slipped into a quantum universe – but to derive greater awareness and presence from the time you have available, hence to become more focused and mindful.

ourselves, we realize how this takes extra courage and confidence. When we next spend some time with someone we care about, switching off the phone, or placing it out of sight, can be one small step towards honouring them. The joy of being silent can pass from you to someone else as easily as a smile – the value of silence ultimately isn't to be measured in words, for this is a contradiction in terms. Rather, to find an inner truth that means something to you, in whatever way seems most appropriate at the time.

COMPASSIONATE FOCUS THERAPY

Through the medium of sound, we share a capacity to resonate with others on an intuitive and proximate level. Through our voice, through our laughter and through the music of our affirmations we can create an environment of positivity.

THIS CHIMES WITH AN UNDERLYING PRINCIPLE of mindfulness – for as we begin to notice our surroundings, we become more observant of others. The sound of us living comes and goes like mist over a lagoon, which serves to remind us our place in the world is impermanent. And yet, these brief echoes of our humanity are the key to the connections we foster with those around us. To live in a world of sound is to validate who or what is creating it; this in turn unlocks our instinct to show compassion.

Compassion, as well as being something we may instinctively feel for ourselves or someone else, also plays a central role in what is known as compassionate focus therapy. In CFT, a therapist explores ways by which a patient can be helped to feel *self*-compassion; once this process is underway, the patient can begin along a path to feeling more resourceful, more able to relate their instincts and responses to their own bank of experiences. This visceral emotional connection is therefore key to one's ability to relate to life's challenges. Without having had the experience of feeling loved or valued, for example, the very concept of love will likely seem abstract, intangible, not something that has any real meaning. So, an ability to connect the responses we feel directly to something in our own experience is central to the notion of compassion. Thought of in this way, CFT need not be solely the province of expert therapists – we can all think more about the tone of voice we use when consoling or supporting others.

Cognitive behavioural therapy, or CBT, concerns itself with the origins of pain and suffering, tapping into myriad complex ways of understanding why we feel what we feel.

'Be kind, for everyone you meet
is fighting a harder battle.'

PLATO (429–347 BCE)

There is an underlying indebtedness to evolution here, by two quite distinct strands: the evolution of human emotions and cognition since the dawn of time, and the evolution of our own individual sense of self. There are countless ways by which cultures, philosophies and religions have attempted to help us make sense of our emotions, drives and instinctive processes. Buddhism is but one among many such ways of thinking about how we might most productively act out our lives. And compassion, in order for it to play its part, is perhaps best understood as being carried along by this complex evolutionary lineage.

As Dr Paul Gilbert, founder of compassionate focus therapy, explains, our thinking and reacting mechanisms are not self-created or evolved, they are the product of countless millennia of subtle transformations over which we have had absolutely no influence whatsoever. Before even beginning to make sense of our emotions and behaviours, let alone what it means to become mindful, Gilbert reminds us we need to take a more pragmatic, realistic view of humanity: 'part of what it means to become mindful is to become mindful of how our brains are made... but *we* didn't make them'.

Compassion for others presumes an acceptance that we are all equally susceptible to the slings and arrows of life, and that, conceptually at least, we have the capacity to place ourselves or our loved ones in the position of others experiencing something undesirable. An ability to place ourselves in some-

one else's shoes is a fundamental component of compassion. It follows that an instinct to empathize or feel compassion for someone else requires us to have the capacity to relate that person's experience to our own; in other words, without self-compassion, feeling compassion for others is unattainable.

Bound up in all this, our own 'genetic expression', as Gilbert refers to it, is almost entirely tied to fortune – or perhaps the lack of it – in respect to things such as physical and mental health predispositions, IQ, geographical or socio-economic factors, and the expectations placed on us by those who have the greatest influence over us. Though none of us can be held responsible for the brains and bodies we were born with, it is still our responsibility to make the best of what we inherited. Therapists use the fact that we all share certain vulnerabilities and weaknesses as a starting point for helping their patients, identifying and acknowledging common ground before tackling specific problems.

For me, the idea that compassion presupposes a capacity for *self*-compassion – coupled with the idea that we can to some extent shape our own future – is invigorating. It's perhaps the opposite of a destiny-based logic, which instantly drains our resolve to overcome the things that threaten to damage or undermine us. This in turn will lead to a sense of empowerment: we can choose to evolve the particular version of ourselves we value most highly – but only by first recognizing the extent to which other less desirable versions

coexist in turmoil within us. Mindfulness is a way of reconciling such dilemmas while honing self-compassion, so that we become more responsive and valuable as citizens. Through sound, we rehearse daily our most powerful way of communicating, and just as importantly, we learn to listen.

Binaural Beats Therapy

Binaural beats therapy is a relatively modern subdivision of sound wave therapy. The basic idea is that we are given a fractionally different tone for each ear, and yet interpret these as one, though in the process a 'beat' is generated by the frequency differential. This differential can be marginal, perhaps just 10 Hz or less, and the overall frequency is considered to be best at under 1 MHz. The sensation has been likened to meditation, and you can purchase readymade audio tracks designed to target a subtly different effect. Binaural beats can be made up of different frequency patterns, each of which is considered to be conducive to a particular state of arousal or relaxation. Delta patterns are apparently helpful for dreamless sleep; Theta patterns have been linked to REM (rapid eye movement), aiding our more inventive side as well as boosting our capacity for meditation; Alpha patterns are said to promote a calm demeanour; and Beta patterns are thought to assist our powers of focus.

Many benefits can be claimed in regard to the binaural beats currently available on the internet, which cover a wide

spectrum of aspects from the relief of anxiety-related disorders to improved concentration, relaxation, attitude of mind and even psychomotor performance. Hence, by no means all people engaging in binaural beats therapy have the same motivation for doing so. There is evidence to suggest that its use, regardless of motivation, is optimal when done in short doses (i.e. under half an hour per day) for more than one month. Following this initial immersive programme, it has been claimed that a person can continue to gain from top-up sessions, especially when used in combination with other more widely used practices, such as meditation. Studies so far are very few in number and draw their provisional conclusions from rather small statistical data sets. Nonetheless, as yet, there seem to have been no reports of binaural beats therapy causing problematic side effects, and this would appear to be an avenue of research worthy of further serious investigation.

A Ringing in the Ears

Tinnitus is a surprisingly common syndrome in which the sufferer experiences a sound not directly caused by an external source – effectively it's the brain working overtime. Tinnitus can take a variety of forms, some more debilitating or enduring than others, including a buzzing, ringing or hissing noise, and it may be intermittent, or appear to come from just one ear. Some people describe the sensation as coming from nowhere specific, a little like toothache can do. The perceived sound can seem so real that the person becomes convinced others must also be able to hear it, or else seem unable to distinguish it from a 'real' sound of a similar sort. These strange sensations can even take the form of a hallucination, or what has been termed 'musical tinnitus', especially if the sufferer is older and has spent a significant amount of their life engaged in some form of musical activity. I've often wondered whether the psychological impact of too much internalized sound could trip a kind of switch in our mind's ear, bringing about a perpetual state of imagined white noise. There are certainly times for me when my imagined hearing takes on a surprisingly high-volume level that I'm not easily able to escape from. If I'm needing to work in a noisy environment, such as an airport or café, it's as though my internal PA system feels the need to crank up the volume in order to smother out extraneous noise. Roughly one person in eight is reported to be a sufferer of prolonged tinnitus, and perhaps triple this number will at some time complain of it over a shorter timescale. Thankfully, many people only get tinnitus as a symptom of a short-lived hearing impairment, such as an ear infection or other remediable ailment.

The relatively high proportion of the population experiencing tinnitus might suggest it stems from something environmental, or perhaps as a result of some kind of life-changing event. Our hearing is so impressively tuned into our immediate sounding environment that our ears need to shut out much of what comes their way as a self-preservation technique. It would be hard for us to make sense of what is important against a backdrop of perpetual din. This explains why it is that an amount of background noise is effectively filtered out without us having to make an effort to do this for ourselves. Hearing experts have deduced that it is when our physical machinery has undergone some kind of alteration, or perhaps injury, that the brain attempts to compensate by ramping up the amount of sound it can acquire from the ears.

Relaxing is a supreme form of medicine for the body and soul

Thought of in this way, tinnitus is often more complex than just a hearing impediment – it can in some circumstances reflect a dip in our resilience to life in general, or else result from a bereavement, prolonged spell of stress or anxiety. This could go some way to explaining why we can sometimes remedy the situation without even trying, simply by allowing ourselves time to let our bodies and minds recalibrate and settle themselves. The British Tinnitus Association explains this process of self-healing as 'habituation' – in other words, we can become acclimatized to the tinnitus in roughly the same way as we might zone out from a buzzing light bulb or vibrating dashboard in our car. It is even thought to be possible to use sound generators to re-educate a sufferer's brain, so that instead of fighting the tinnitus they become inured to it.

The relevance of this is that we can be shown ways to self-heal tinnitus, to at least some degree, by calming down our body and mind. Relaxing, put simply, is a supreme form of medicine for the body and soul – through a state of heightened tranquillity we can acquire the capacity to blot out these unwanted distractions. Paying heed to the sensation of air being drawn slowly into our lungs, and then flowing out again, can be enough to help us 'park' tinnitus somewhere where it is less harmful or frustrating. Another form of self-help can be introducing an 'actual' background sound into your life if tinnitus worsens. This drowns out the perceived sound, leaving us feeling less encumbered by it – if you experience tinnitus from time to time, you might experiment with soothing, meditative or natural sounds (or even suitably soporific music) to see if this alleviates the problem a little.

A useful mindfulness tool addresses tinnitus by simply 'giving in' to the sound that is causing havoc in the head; instead of attempting to smother it, the sufferer can be shown how to accept the sound's right to exist; by refraining from confronting the internal sound we become open to a palette of more healthy awareness, which goes beyond sound and utilizes the other senses. By refocusing our mind on our sense of smell, touch or sight, for example, the impact of tinnitus can be mollified. This technique effectively places a safety zone between the harmful effects of tinnitus and our power to become slowly reconciled to it.

CHAPTER FOUR

DEEP LISTENING

To listen is to observe through the medium of sound, and hence to make a timely difference to our relationships by showing compassion and understanding. Listening is also a tool to help us tune in to the physical space we are in, and at the same time help others to feel more empowered and engaged. We get to choose how deeply we wish to listen, since the sound is always there, some of it consonant, some dissonant, waiting to ignite sensations and spark our curiosity.

THE TIPPING-POINT OF SOUND AND MUSIC

◆

The next time you hear a field mouse scurry off into the hedgerow, you might ask yourself, is this music? If by music we are referring to the involuntary physical vibrations of the air, then a Martian might find little to distinguish between, say, a beetle and The Beatles.

WHEN WE STOP TO MARVEL AT HOW Vivaldi captured the essence of falling autumn leaves in his timeless work, 'The Four Seasons', or how the jazz singer, Nat King Cole, came at the same challenge from an entirely different angle with 'Autumn Leaves' more than two centuries later, we glimpse at an age-old tradition of depicting aspects of the natural world through music. An inventory of musicians who have done something along vaguely similar lines might look endless – Vaughan Williams's 'Sea Symphony', 'The Green, Green Grass of Home', as sung by Tom Jones, Mussorgsky's 'A Night on the Bare Mountain', or 'I Can See Clearly Now' performed by Johnny Nash.

While some of these examples seem little more than clichéd flirtations with nature, others perhaps come closer to an attempt at metaphorical representation. A common denominator among them, it seems to me, is not so much an encouragement to parody or satirize, but to suspend belief, even for a few minutes, that the world is not intrinsically un-musical; or perhaps the reverse even, that music is not intrinsically un-worldly? The French composer, Saint-Saëns, achieved what might be the best-known caricature of all in his 'Carnival of the Animals' – the cuckoo is represented by an off-stage clarinet, birds by flutes, an elephant by double-basses and the swan by a cello. But the success of Saint-Saëns's admittedly humorous portrayal relies heavily on our need to humanize before we can begin to empathize. What seems to me most striking about Saint-Saëns's iconic work, aside from its enduring attractiveness as a piece of Western art music, is how cunningly he taps into the confirmation bias of listeners, regardless of age – often by focusing on the speed and/or pitch register of these animals rather than by attempting to emulate their sound in literal ways. Take the tortoise, for example – apart from hissing and panting occasionally, the tortoise makes no noise at all – nor of course do fish swimming in an aquarium (let alone fossils, which are depicted by a xylophone).

Contrast this with how a painter might pursue a similarly flimsy rustic 'brief' – artists can easily convince us with their vision of the natural world, if they so wish, since the degree of realism or abstraction they employ is entirely up to them. A skilled painter can make a swan look like a swan or a tortoise look like a tortoise in ways even Saint-Saëns could never achieve through the medium of tonal music. If we compare Jackson Pollock's 'Autumn Rhythm' with Claude Monet's 'Autumn on the Seine' and George Inness's 'Autumn Oaks' we see three very different solutions to the challenge of preserving something of autumn through the medium of canvas.

Through the medium of music (something we generally 'know' we are hearing, even if no two people would likely agree exactly what 'good' music is), we are often presented with a sincere if at times naïve scintilla of the physical world. In all the above musical examples, it would of course be entirely possible to enjoy the music without the faintest idea that its lyrics or instrumental effects bear any of the aforementioned worldly/animal allusions. Though so-called 'programme music', which is guided by a narrative or allegory, might be what motivated a composer to create a piece of music, the fact is that for those not in the know, this aspect could just as easily disappear under the radar.

Unless we dip more than just a tentative toe into the possibilities for combining worldly sounds with 'real' music, we perhaps delude ourselves that there is anything but a random relationship between the sounds our world makes and the structured, manipulated patterns we humans find so irresistible. The milieu known as 'biomusic' (see chapter 1) records

---

'If you look deep enough you will see music; the heart of nature being everywhere music.'

THOMAS CARLYLE (1795–1881)
PHILOSOPHER, WRITER, HISTORIAN

---

real animals (or plants), either alone or combined with human music. Whale noises have proved perhaps as popular as birdsong in this genre, an example being American avant-garde composer George Crumb's 'Vox Balaenae'.

The great nineteenth-century German philosopher, Arthur Schopenhauer, invested considerable intellectual energy in reconsidering the phenomenal ('real') world and metaphysical world (more specifically for Schopenhauer, the idea that animals, vegetables and minerals share common aspects with human will). After just a fleeting dip into Schopenhauer's *The World as Will and Representation*, we cannot fail to applaud the grand enterprise of Schopenhauer's speculations.

In a recent controversial experiment, the bioacoustics specialist, Monica Gagliano, endeavoured to provide evidence that plants communicate with each other by means of vegetal vibrations. According to the American musicologist and writer, Holly Watkins, in her strikingly original book, *Musical Vitalities*, Gagliano's research on plant vibrations (not normally audible by humans) used amplification and auto-tuning techniques. Though potentially an area worthy of further study, there is perhaps a danger we could come away imagining that plants communicate with each other in ways that share similarities with humans. In contrast, it is interesting to reflect upon Schopenhauer's romanticised portrayal of plants as autonomous organisms, which by such definition have little need for communication.

To stretch this idea in another, perhaps more provocative direction still, the idea that plants respond to human voices is one that has fascinated us for the longest time. In a study by the Royal Horticultural Society (RHS), it was revealed that women's voices can have a particularly advantageous effect on the growth pattern of plants compared with men's voices. Works of literature were read to plants 'wearing' headphones over the period of one month. This extends Charles Darwin's tentative proposal made back in the nineteenth century that plants grow in response to vibration – a hypothesis that, alas, he failed to demonstrate by getting his son to play the bassoon in proximity to certain plants. In light of the promising RHS research, perhaps there is scope to study plant growth in response to a broader range of musical instruments in order to expand on the provisional success enjoyed by female speakers?

Whatever we feel about a relationship that may or may not exist between human will and the world that is physically and undeniably *there* everywhere we look, it is certainly attractive to reimagine music as having resonances with some emerging subdisciplines of life science. Schopenhauer did not, Watkins cautions, feel that 'tenors sounded like trees, nor altos like asps', but was attempting to illustrate by analogy that the rising registers of human voices – basses, tenors, altos and sopranos – have a broadly plausible parallel with 'natural enti- ties'. A contemporary aesthetics of nature might do well, Watkins seems to suggest, to celebrate what remains of the

world not yet irredeemably contaminated by human inter-
vention and planet abuse. And, more than this, we might
occasionally remind ourselves how Schopenhauer's philoso-
phy of the world and our place within it can still have
resonance for us in this modern age, in which we increasingly
speak of conservation and ecology more volubly than we do
wonderment or simple beauty. This final point holds especial
significance for those whose interest in mindfulness extends
to an ambition for a more harmonious natural world.

The tipping-point of sound and music is inevitably tied in
with our personal evaluation of the function and meaning of
natural sound – not just of plants and vegetation, but of other
animals and the elements. The edge between these will not
become less fuzzy by humanizing what is not human, however
tempting it may be to do this, but through our ability to grasp
natural sound in a more mindful, if not necessarily spiritual
way. Both Darwin and Schopenhauer, who were direct con-
temporaries, had a deep admiration for the natural world,
even if they chose to set about understanding it or explaining
it in rather contrasting ways. We can all marvel at a chorus of
seagulls flying overhead, or the optimistic banter we imagine
is taking place between chickens in our back yard as we
approach bearing food, without becoming distracted by the
mechanisms by which they do this. I'm not at all sure I know
what a fragile ecosystem *sounds* like, any more than a buoyant
one. Nor do I feel obligated to elevate the harmonious noises

of new-born babies above the sound of a falling tree or a rattle snake readying itself for attack. These sounds have no intrinsic hierarchy, only perhaps their own empirical value for each of us, to help us make sense of what enters our ears.

The point is, our sense and sensibilities as humans give us an unrivalled capacity for showing the world compassion, for savouring its sounds and drawing inspiration from them. As we walk through a wood, breaking branches underfoot and whistling capriciously into the echoing hillside, we are contributing to the very sounds someone picnicking nearby can use mindfully, either there and then or perhaps later as they replay it in the form of a meditation track on their phone. We don't need a definition of sound any more than we need a definition of music in order to derive value, pleasure or inspiration from hearing it. Mindfulness is one of the ways we can demonstrate this simplest of ideas for ourselves, every day.

We don't need a definition of sound in order to derive value or inspiration from it

A Tapestry of Sound

If a tapestry is a picture that has been woven into cloth, what then is a tapestry of sound? It strikes me that virtually every environment, whether it be subterranean, at the earth's surface or high up in some stratospheric Alpine range, has its own uniquely intricate sound texture – the sound equivalent to a piece of tapestry, in which threads of sound interlace and spur off at various points. The fact that one is the product of painstaking skill and the other occurs naturally matters no more than if we were to compare the sound of an Alpine wind with, say, Richard Strauss's 'Alpine Symphony'. We can choose whether to allow each sound environment, human-made or not, to wash over us, rather like a sound installation artist might invite us to do in a more formal setting, or to pick away at the individual sounds until they reveal their particular identity. This, not unlike the work of a sound analyst or engineer, effectively de-randomizes the sound by isolating its discernible voices or characters, so that, just like homing in on individual voices in a crowd, a new level of intelligibility emerges.

The Bayeux Tapestry, a supreme example of embroidery from the eleventh century depicting the Norman Conquest, is a feast for the eye; at 70 metres in length it could take some time to soak in the narrative. How many different strands of *sound* might you hear if you were to amble over a similar distance, eyes closed? The homogeneity of a piece of tapestry and a naturally occurring tapestry of sound, presents us with countless options as we slowly lose ourselves somewhere deep within it. The act of listening in this way isn't so much about analysis or interrogation as allowing our point of focus to shift at will, in the same way as we might marvel at a scene in the tapestry depicting warring troops one minute, but then zoom in on a minuscule fragment of exquisite detail the next.

CHAPTER FIVE

THE SOUND OF SPEECH

*Rhythm and algorithm are tangled up
in every sentence we utter. Even when meaning
becomes clouded by the paraphernalia of more playful
language, we can savour its sincerity and smile at its
ambiguity. The tonal palette of someone speaking to
us in an unfamiliar language will still convey a
smattering of their personality. The point of speech
is partly about communication, but surely at
least as much about exchanging aloof emotional
messages to remind us we are human.*

SOUND AND MEMORY

◆

When we see a person whom we think we recognize, it will be the tone of their voice that clinches it. We wrap the two identities – the visual and the auditory – so tightly together that they become one. The visual aspects of a person are illusory – haircuts and facial aging alters appearances hugely – but how a person sounds is a more visceral route to their soul.

EACH OF US HAS A UNIQUE SONIC FINGERPRINT – this is not merely a composite of our physical attributes, voice box, mouth shape, sex, age and so on – but reflects the intricate baggage of social and cultural experiences that we bring to that voice. It is with this voice that we may join with others in search of community; in this sense, the notion that the people have 'a voice' is not so fantastical, since it chimes easily with the idea of a shared resonance, both physical and emotional.

Sound memory occurs, not unlike other forms of memory, through repetition. It may be tempting to imagine we archive sounds similar to the way this is done on the hard drive of a computer – such as sounds captured as MP3 or WAV files perhaps, or images as JPEG or PDF files. Importantly however, there would appear to be a plasticity to the way neutrons in the brain's auditory cortex achieve effective memory, making the brain infinitely more adaptable and versatile than any computer. It is worth reflecting that there is no way of

storing the *actual* smell or taste of, say, a banana onto a computer, even though its chemical makeup can of course be stored just as any other data set.

In recent studies from France, participants presented with different sound patterns managed to recall them accurately two weeks later without too much difficulty, even when the number of repetitions had been limited to perhaps just two. The plasticity assumed to be present from these provisional studies is supported by the observation that humans can often quickly relearn a sound that was once familiar to them (such as after suffering a stroke or hearing loss), and also that there is a high level of association between, say, the sound of a person's voice and the face that goes with it. The phrase 'it's good to put a face to the name' is common, and yet without an ability to put a face to a *voice* our powers of recognition would be a whole lot less dependable. It may also be the case that a slowly failing ability in one of these capabilities can be compensated for in the other.

Another reason our brains are significantly different from a computer's hard drive is the speed and agility with which the storing mechanism itself can adapt. Sounds, it seems, are stored on the fly, memorized by lightning-quick auditory plasticity – imagine a hard drive that can reshape its own storing mechanism to accommodate minute details. Patterns are easier to memorize, and sequences are also relatively easily captured compared with more random sound events.

Recognizing Speech

Speech recognition is not the same as speech comprehension, as anyone setting foot in an unknown foreign land will be all too aware of. And yet, somehow, we still immediately know we are hearing a spoken language by means of vocal tones, vowels, consonants and myriad other inflections, maybe with similarities to our own language. We might even be able to mimic the sounds with a degree of accuracy, too – without understanding a single word.

Similarly, perhaps, a person might be able to detect or even replicate the pitch of a note played by a musical instrument without being able to distinguish which instrument it was played on. Incidentally, we presume a capacity to detect we are hearing a real voice, as opposed to a computer-generated one, and yet this in itself requires a high level of plasticity and responsiveness. It has been noticed that when a particular sound is repeated, the brain quickly detects this and loosens its focus correspondingly in order to direct it more purposefully elsewhere. This can also aid the detection of one voice from another, as opposed to the individual components of particular words, such as consonants and vowels (and the subdivisions of these also).

> *Anyone setting foot in an unknown land still immediately knows when they are hearing a spoken language*

PHONETICS AND PHONOLOGY

Phonetics is the study of the sounding word — how each component of it is formed in the mouth (or indeed elsewhere, such as the throat, nasal cavities and sinus), pronounced and actually brought to life from its static representation on a page.

EMBRACING SIGN LANGUAGE, phonetics falls within the field of descriptive linguistics; it also deals with how such sounds or signs are perceived. If each written word presents a range of theoretical possibilities for how it might sound, phonetics is its sounding reality. Phonetics does not in any case discriminate between languages as such — it is essentially just a way of categorizing the most common sounds within a range familiar to the reader — so one could conceive of phonetic analysis being applied to a randomly invented mumbo-jumbo language. And when we consider how a range of regional or world accents 'legitimately' skews the sounding components of many words, the possibilities for 'correct' pronunciation become far, far greater than the most comprehensive phonetic tome could do justice to. Interpretation therefore becomes an inescapable aspect of phonetics — the song 'Let's Call the Whole Thing Off' by George and Ira Gershwin, has the line 'You like tomato and I like tom-mah-to' (tə'meɪte/tə 'maxtə), a comical illustration of how cultural factors can significantly alter how the same word is pronounced.

Phonology, on the other hand, which is a subset of linguistics, tackles the *meaning* trapped in the words, not just how they sound. Phonology is about analysing and categorizing patterns within a particular language and hence how to make sense of them from the standpoint of a person familiar with that language. While a phoneticist is concerned with how and why words or syllables sound as they do, a phonologist seeks to derive significance from these sounds, placing greater importance on one aspect than another.

Chanting and Mantras

Mantras are repeated vocal sounds used to help us access deeper inside ourselves. As the tongue makes contact with the palate, we are thought to be releasing a cocktail of chemicals to the brain and body, which in turn can have healing properties. In a practical sense, a mantra sets up a mechanism by which we may gradually zone out of the distracting thoughts that hinder meditation and mindfulness. This heightened state of mental focus is ideal for calming the body and mind; it also frees up our tendency to overthink and interrogate. What's more, emotions which creep in unwanted during meditation will cause us either to attempt to smother them or engage in conflict with them; irrespective of which is happening, this is the opposite to what we are endeavouring to achieve. The act of chanting a mantra is a way of channelling such emotions or stories away from us, leaving us unfettered and ready to be

more serene. Just as a particular tone of voice or piece of music has the power to alter our sense of wellbeing, the subtlest vibrations in the chanting voice can be taught to resonate down and up the body, causing it to feel more ready to experience the benefits of mindfulness.

Some imagine that the vibrations in their physical bodies belong to a particular quality of life, such as love or happiness. Through mantras we can access these by purposefully 'vibrating' them — it is as if we *become* the vibration through the act of chanting it. Furthermore, we can alter our emotional state by consciously altering the vibration. But chanting is not as easy as it sounds — it can take considerable time and patience to lock onto a pace of breathing which brings about this desired sense of detachment from outside noises and thoughts. And when it comes to mastering Gurmukhi (a sacred script employed in Kundalini yoga), let alone Sanskrit, it is not hard to see why spiritual learning is a long-term endeavour.

Chanting is most effective when done over a longer time period, perhaps several hours. This is something best built up slowly and patiently, as is the case with silent meditation. For the deeper the physical vibration, the more healing and beneficial the *emotional* vibration that is said to come with it. We might feel a loss of alignment, or else sense there are places located in specific regions of our body where vibration is not as good; these can be targeted by choosing a mantra that fits best with it. Each limb is taught patiently to rejuvenate itself.

The focal points located in the 'subtle body' (in mystical teaching, a psycho-spiritual aspect which complements others in the 'great chain of being' that we commonly refer to as our physical presence as human beings) are known as 'chakras'. Chakras play a pivotal role in meditation and yoga. In Hinduism, as well as Buddhism, we find references to between five and seven chakras (for example the throat and heart), each having their own specific type of vibration, which in turn is stimulated by a particular mantra.

While yoga practitioners may feel that chanting a mantra elevates us from a physical to a sacred state, it need not be the case that chanting has such religious connotations. We may feel it is sufficient to enter a secular emotional state, as distinct from a numinous one ('a mysterious or awe-inspiring religious emotion'). The complexity of a mantra, whether iterated in Sanskrit or more

We might harmonize our mind and body with the help of a mantra

modern language from India or elsewhere, elevates it to a deeply philosophical level, which will best be learned with the help of a teacher. We may feel that it is enough simply to know that we might harmonize our mind and body with the help of such a sound. But guidance will be needed if you wish to translate accurately the words of a particular mantra, and indeed if you wish to be shown which one might be of especial help to you along your spiritual journey.

An example of a mantra is *Sat Nam*, meaning 'The truth is my name'. You may be surprised at how specific we are supposed to be when chanting it in order to derive spiritual and physical value from doing so. For now, we might follow the guide that *Sat* (pronounced *Saaaaaaat*) needs to be eight times the length or emphasis of *Nam*. It is believed that when incorporated into the 'Sat Kriya' meditation it can stimulate sexual potency, but only if sustained for three minutes on a daily basis. It has been suggested that your entire spine can be set into vibration through the Sat Nam mantra, if the *Sat* is ideally thirty-five times as long as the *Nam*.

The Om

The *Om* (pronounced A-U-M) mantra is surely the best known of all, though it can be deceptively tricky to learn, especially as an almost continuous inwardly throbbing sound. Widely believed to be the first sound ever to have been heard in our universe, chanting the Om encapsulates both the meditative resonance needed to give it spiritual meaning and the most precise dovetailing of physical and philosophical states imaginable. Surprisingly, though the Om presents as the simplest two-letter word when on paper, you'll quickly see how all-encompassing and potentially valuable it can be if you are able to emulate the sound of a Tibetan monk sat high on a hill. Don't be concerned if you can't muster a deep, impressively booming Om. You'll find claims on the internet that a

MINDFULNESS EXERCISE

CHANT THE OM

Begin by sitting calmly on the floor, perhaps with your legs crossed in a gentle fold (a half lotus position). Alternatively, sit on a chair with one leg crossed at ninety degrees over the other – what's important is that you feel comfortable. Your arms can relax in your lap or assume an upward cupped hand position. Now slowly calm yourself and close your eyes as you turn your point of mental focus to your breathing. You won't be settled enough to begin straight away.

A good Om takes roughly ten seconds to unfold, followed by a further ten seconds of silence:

a-ā-u-ū-m-ng . . . followed by about ten seconds of silence to breathe and prepare.

Imagine, as you form the first two syllables (a-ā-), that your mouth is so wide open it could almost hold the entire universe. For the next two syllables (u-ū-) it may help to purse your lips as you direct your sound from as deep inside you as you can muster. The final two syllables of the six (m-ng…) are for me the trickiest because the sound needs to continue to resonate while your tongue rests without pressure on the roof of your mouth. Some people like to allow their teeth to vibrate during this final phase. Don't rush to inhale and start a new Om; let each one reverberate from the base of your pelvis up through to the top of your head, so that with each emission you feel progressively more tranquil as you move from a physical to mystical state. Doing the Om (euphemistically known as 'Oming') is supposedly most effective when done 108 times, because this opens one's Path to Self-Realization. There are 108 prayer beads in a garland or 'Malas', and several intriguing reasons the number holds significance in Hinduism and yoga.

particular pitch, such as 417 Hz, is best for your Om to help you 'unblock' or 'cleanse' your soul. But the important thing is to find your own note that you can return to many times without straining your voice.

Incantations

An incantation is generally taken to mean a form of magical bewitchery or spell that can be chanted, sung or spoken, either by a witch, wizard or fairy. Incantations, also known as 'enchantments', overlapped in their various ways with several main religions before eventually being wiped out due to out-moded connotations of sorcery and evil deeds. The highly specific use and emphasis of words and rhymes is said to lead to different outcomes directly following an incantation, and much meaning is derived from the patterning of such words during a ritual. In an incantation there is frequently an under-lying implication of a magical act being imposed upon someone (or something) by someone else.

Though so-called magic words, such as 'abracadabra' and 'hocus pocus', have become threaded into a vast, overlapping literature spanning many centuries and cultures, the precise meanings of such 'pseudo-Latin' words seem often only to be shared among those privy to such esoteric knowledge. Either that, or the words never had meaning in the first place, but rather were calculated to sound mystical and loaded with dark, supernatural meaning.

It has been observed that the formulaic presentation of incantations, and their repetitive nature, leaves them faintly resembling the hypnotic effect of a Sanskrit mantra, though the underlying meanings could hardly be more different. The colourful evocation of snake charmers in the East survives to this day, as does the use of live snakes within certain forms of meditation and chanting. Indeed, India's fascination for snakes goes back perhaps thousands of years, as does the realization that though snakes do not have ears, their entire bodies can resonate to the sound of a wooden flute.

Tone, Meaning and Conciliation

We can draw a connection between sound, meaning and conciliation in regard to the tone of voice we use to communicate with others. Is the sound of our voice – its pitch, volume, inflection, speed – designed to be of maximum value to the person we are communicating with, or have we allowed it to mirror some negative ego that lives inside us? If so, the tone of our words may well impact more greatly than the words themselves. The internalized tone of voice we instinctively use when turning over a sensitive topic in our mind should ideally match the tone we use when expressing our opinion to someone else. This achieves two things: firstly, we will be channelling our instinct for self-compassion into compassion for someone else; secondly, we will be tapping into the best, most positive version of ourselves we know we are capable of.

When an argument is getting out of control, sometimes a conscious change to your tone of voice can transport you somewhere more conciliatory; through mindful management of sound, the desire to recover common ground then becomes a stronger impulse than to win the argument at all costs. Sound is an incredibly powerful tool, at least as powerful as the words to which it becomes attached. When we seek to soothe an animal, or a very small child, we may well be able to achieve this by managing our tone in a thoughtful way, even when the content of our words bears no relation to the calmness we are projecting. Conversely, one could make a recipe for apple pie sound more like a declaration of war by adopting a loud, assertive, unrelentingly high-pitched tone.

What a Lie Sounds Like

It's interesting to probe a little more deeply into how a particular sound can trigger a reaction in us. Just as a baby's crying immediately mobilizes us – we simply cannot ignore it – it turns out there are other sounds which have been 'designed' to cause us to react in certain ways. Coupled with this, it appears that animals as well as humans have evolved an impressive range of sounds which they call upon routinely to manipulate others of their species. Ulterior motives, it would seem, are not solely the province of humans.

I heard zoologist Lucy Cooke discussing this intriguing topic on a radio programme entitled *The Power of Deceit*. The

programme explored the idea that sound can be used as a form of deception for an animal's own ends. Camouflage isn't just about disguising the visual dimension of a living thing, which of course happens plentifully in nature, from snakes and other reptiles to insects, fish and others – it's also about manipulating *sound*. So, what does a lie sound like? Surely for a lie to sound plausible, at least two conditions need to be met: firstly, the content of the lie needs to be sustainable, and secondly the tone of the delivery needs to match what it would be if true. An amusing example of this is the farmyard cock, who knows exactly how to mimic the sound of food being delivered with its 'cluck'. He can use this to his advantage by encouraging the females to follow him, when all along he had something else on his mind: sex.

The idea that animals are not habitually disingenuous was something most of us once bought into; after all, monogamy was a central premise of Darwin – until, that is, Richard Dawkins dared to upturn our naïvety in his groundbreaking book *The Selfish Gene* (1976). The continued success of a species, including human beings, was at one time thought to be self-regulating – it was assumed that certain members of the community would, for example, selflessly refrain from procreation for the greater good in times when overpopulation seemed imminent. But the flaw in this is that it underestimates those members of a community who are motivated by selfish desires. An interesting question is, therefore, to what

extent are such behaviours cognitive, i.e. contrived by an animal/human to get its way over matters of food or sex, or else simply part of the hardwiring itself? Primates, not unlike humans, are more than capable of deceiving each other in order to garner or hoard those things that are most treasured, but this could be explained in terms of pragmatic or even involuntary acts, as opposed to tactical, staged manoeuvres.

That being said, we humans use deceit, at least at some level, on a daily basis. The notion of a 'white lie', used as a gambit to sustain a harmonious existence with our fellow human beings, is perhaps not one we would want to own up to, and yet without the skill of doing this, an uneasy truth will quickly undermine social niceties and lead to hurt feelings. Curiously, it would seem we have become better at lying than in *detecting* a lie, so that only those who are 'professional' liars, such as criminals or actors, outperform chance when it comes to telling a fibber from a truth teller. This surely tells us as much about the ability to weigh up tonal meaning as visual cues, such as scratching an ear or not looking you in the eye.

CHAPTER SIX

SOUNDSCAPES

*A landscape is a scenic vista — an expansive
horizon that draws our eye as we peer out from a
skyscraper; or a rugged mountain range best viewed
from horseback. What, then, is a soundscape? To me,
a soundscape is more than just the easily quantifiable
parts of an acoustic ecology, or some fleeting immersion
in natural sound. It is the noise-music of a crowded
office, or the near-silent panorama of a dormant
volcano; a celebration in sound of living and
not yet living space.*

CITYSCAPES

◆

The sound of a city that never sleeps is either enthralling or intimidating, depending on which side of the tracks you happen to live on. No city ever sleeps, it just pauses for long enough to restock its shelves with cooking oil and cigarettes.

THERE ARE CERTAIN URBAN LANDSCAPES, New York undoubtedly among them, which give a good impression of being comfortable in their own skin, even at 4 am. The skylines of Chicago, Tokyo and Hong Kong trace out a kind of histogram of ambition, their high-rises blending in uneasily with adjacent tenderloin areas colourfully self-styled to distract us from their darker side. Other more compact cities, such as Singapore, Venice or Stockholm, may appear perpetually drenched in a watery sunset. All conurbations are plausible emblems of a unique social history, each with its own bespoke soundscape of street life, car horns, wine bars and sirens. Every commuter-land trumpets out its own sound DNA; the unique hustlebustle of a community perpetually on the move, on the up or on the make.

And then there are cities like Dhaka or Kolkata, where the heat and haste of opposing traffic collide to form an unmistakable, intoxicating soundscape. In Amsterdam and Paris, city workers reluctantly yield to a hubbub of trains, taxis and trams. All this intricate metal spaghetti connects the working to the sleeping; the city is home to those who have places to go, but also for those whose get-up-and-go has got-up-and-gone. The pulsating heart of a partying town like Ayia Napa, Cyprus, tramples over the somnolent yawns of the weary. On the other hand, for some, the bright lights can never be bright enough, nor the music loud enough. As morning shift workers trade places with the night crew awaiting the red-eye bus home, the relentless beat of urban life can seem soulless. This same concrete jungle is also home to those whose resting place is confined to a shop doorway.

Every modern city moves to its own peculiar groove. Its hodgepodge of hipster cafés and upmarket pizza joints sustain thinkers, doers and pretenders of every conceivable denomination. Once night falls, a city that may be owned by the over-fifties in the daytime better resembles an urban playground for the under thirties. But this is a form of power-sharing most of us unwittingly sign up to. A cityscape is an embodiment of our collective ambitions, achievements and shortcomings; an organic mélange of sound which, just like us, is always changing and evolving. We tell ourselves we are part of a community whose values we share, though we may never speak to more than a tiny handful as we jostle for position amid the silent panic of the morning rush hour.

LIVING MINDFULLY IN THE CITY

◆

How are we to live mindfully in a city that commands our attention every time we dash across a road or stand on tiptoes to hail a cab? Realistically, we may never find our oasis of calm, however hard we look. Living mindfully in the city is not about remodelling its bricks into a temple of peace, more about redefining our relationship to it.

CITY NOISE ISN'T AN ABERRATION or a continuous impudent two-fingered gesture, it's proof we are all still here, alive and hoping to live a little longer. Silence in a city might in any case seem deafening to a dweller who gets off to sleep to the lullaby of night delivery trucks. Perhaps we don't need silence anyway – better to find our peace within the noise, rather than try to smother it out or overwhelm it with a noise of our own choosing. For many folks, a solution of sorts comes from listening to music or watching videos as they journey around their city, clutching their coffee.

But tactics such as these merely cut us off from the communities we say we love. It's a form of denial, and as with all forms of denial it is the person doing the denying who ultimately pays the price. Besides, when our devices run out of power, we too feel disempowered. There was once a time when an unguarded rustle of newspapers was frowned upon in a public place and, later, when a ringtone would have brought a carriage full of passengers to a catatonic rage. But this tells us more about spurious time-stamped notions of acceptable behaviour than it does about the sound itself. We could enforce silent train carriages, libraries and hospitals if we really insisted, but we'd probably just end up living in a state of hushed anguish. Silence, in these terms, can actually seem more a form of oppression than conducive of a positive state of being. If you can function just as creatively sitting in a busy student canteen as when alone in a field full of swaying lavender, I'd say you have reached a kind of enlightenment.

Imagine the city is just another living organism, easing its way forward through time as best it can. Thought of in this way, city noise becomes city *life* which, just like us, deserves to be noticed, recognized, loved and valued. Learning to embrace sound, even when it wasn't asked for, is a first step towards feeling free of persecution from it. Remind yourself that you probably wouldn't want to live in a city that is silent.

'This City now doth, like a garment, wear
The beauty of the morning; silent, bare,
Ships, towers, domes, theatres and temples lie
Open unto the fields and to the sky;
All bright and glittering in the smokeless air.'

FROM 'UPON WESTMINSTER BRIDGE'
IN 'POEMS IN TWO VOLUMES' BY WILLIAM WORDSWORTH
(LONGMAN, HURST, REES AND ORMS, LONDON, 1807)

For in protecting yourself from screaming babies and belligerent one-sided phone conversations you'd also be denied the chance to eavesdrop on a delightful story being told to an infant, or the sudden spectacle of a train performer who has learned to handstand while singing 'The Saints go Marching in'. We can't filter out undesirable sounds before they reach our ears, nor could we reach a consensus of what undesirable really means. But with practice we can become more adept at allowing sound to wash over us; no harm done.

There is nothing malevolent about sound itself; there may be occasions when we imagine a sound has singled us out because it knows we will be especially damaged by it, but this is just us attempting to make sense of the nonsensical. That sound would have happened even if we'd not been there. The noise police have no jurisdiction in a city; besides, if we lost our hearing for just one minute we would surely savour every cough and sneeze that blasts by us for the rest of that day.

Each of us contributes to the sound of the city

A city can only function as a city if we allow it to express its ephemeral identity through the 'language' of sound. Rarely will it make sense, but nor was it designed to. Sound will carry on regardless of our interpretation or admonishment of it, irrespective of how loudly we attempt to counter it internally. And besides, each of us contributes to this language of the city, adding subtly to the meaning of the moment. Accepting and noticing sound is the opposite of judging it or labelling it. Resistance to unsolicited sound is futile, whereas allowing ourselves to play an active role within it, out loud or tacitly, would seem a more profitable way of understanding the nature of sound, and living mindfully in the city.

GREENSCAPES

To commune with nature is to remind yourself you are a creature, too. An amble through shaded pastureland, where the cracking of bark under foot echoes like fireworks for miles around, is rejuvenating in ways not easily expressed, even by poets, painters or composers.

THE COUNTRYSIDE IS A REMINDER of our collective heritage. It gives us a fanciful glimpse of what the world might have resembled had we not interfered with it. If we take a stroll through fields and meadows, before long we find ourselves listening in ways we generally cannot when tugged by the infernal din of engineering, phone babble and transportation. We slowly recalibrate our ears and begin to appreciate the kinds of sounds our earliest ancestors might have heard, six million years ago. We notice convivial conversations between birds and how the wind affects certain types of tree more than others. We notice those sounds that rekindle a connection with the natural world we first experienced when we were small. We don't all live near a wooded clearing or forest glade, but we can make the most of whatever moments of tranquillity our particular landscape presents to us. This might more closely resemble a motionless desert, or a frantically congested metropolis, than a lush, emerald woodland. And yet, this hardly matters; it is what we take away with us afterwards that is ultimately valuable, not where we may have spent the afternoon denuding our mind of its clutter. We probably have a less hectic physical space we can go, wherever we live in the world, and with a little imagination this can become our oasis of calm. Moreover, it is interesting to see how effortlessly a rural and urban setting can blur into each other, particularly from the prospective of sound.

We might imagine that at the first opportunity town folk would rise up from their desks and launch themselves head-long at the countryside, hankering after the tiniest patch of green. But if we peel away at the somewhat romantic stereo-type of the city being somewhere where money is made, and the country where we prefer to spend our leisure time, we

---

'The lowest and vilest alleys of London do
not present a more dreadful record of sin than does the
smiling and beautiful countryside.'

FROM 'THE ADVENTURES OF SHERLOCK HOLMES' BY ARTHUR CONAN DOYLE
(GEORGE NEWNES, LONDON, 1892)

---

quickly find contradictions. For some, the idea of retiring to a little place in the country with hills off in the distance, a little stream trickling at the bottom of the garden, the sound of birds and bees the only things breaking the silence, is nothing short of a horror story.

On a warm Sunday afternoon during my first trip to Hong Kong, following advice from my travel guide, I took a saunter through the main park, a wonderful toll-free space within an easy stroll of the Mass Transit Railway station and Star Ferry terminal. I expected to find every blade of grass occupied by city dwellers clamouring for an hour or two's relief from the frenzy of another working week crammed together in air-conditioned offices on The Island. I also imagined there would be an amount of ball playing, dog-walking and picnicking, as well as excited parents watching youngsters take their first ever wobble on a bicycle. Instead, I found I had the entire place virtually to myself, complete with Tai Chi garden, aviary, lake, exotic plants, statues and trees. Where is every-one, I kept asking myself in disbelief?

As I exited through Cotton Tree Drive an hour or so later, I immediately found myself surrounded by large groups of women, sitting and talking, eating, cooking, dancing, beading each other's hair and thoroughly enjoying themselves. The delightful raucousness of their laughter and music easily swamped the nearby chaos of car horns and high-pitched mopeds chicaning their way through the busy streets of

Central. I later discovered that these women were maids and nannies, hired by the Hong Kongers from the Philippines and Indonesia, making the most of their Sunday off. But instead of congregating in the park as I might have guessed, they chose to occupy every available corner of paving stone for as far as the eye could see.

As I look back on that day, I no longer feel the bewilderment of my encounter. For these women, I now realize, it wasn't the noise and bustle they were trying to escape from, it was the routine and isolation of their work. They hardly seemed to notice the perpetual stream of pedestrians detouring around them, for they had successfully tuned out everyone who was not a part of their joyful micro community. Integral to this was the shared sound of their exuberance and feeling of inclusion, the playful noise of uncensored contentment.

The sense of freedom we might feel when we walk through wide-open spaces is perhaps as much to do with what is missing as what we actually see before us. A pastoral paradise is denuded of manufactured objects of desire, uncluttered by those things we draw comfort from when sat at home. It may take us a while to reacquaint our eyes to the wildlife working its magic up in the trees, and our ears may not be sufficiently fine-tuned to marvel at that flock of birds hurtling by overhead as if in a race to reach the third cloud from the right.

SEASCAPES

The sea has not been poured from some vessel in the sky for our entertainment or edification; covering 70 per cent of its total surface, from above, you could almost say the sea 'is' the world. And in it, another world exists, in which ambition and earthly delights thankfully have no value at all.

I LIVE NOT TOO FAR FROM THE SEA, a stone's throw from the most southwestern corner of England – a small, picturesque town called St Ives. Despite its reticulation of tiny, crisscrossing roads and cobbled streets, the town punches above its weight as a historical fishing port. It is just seven miles away from Penzance to the south, and yet on the opposite coast. Just catching a glimpse of the sea as you drive along a coastal route is enough to place you in a peaceful, more positive frame of mind, admiring seagulls doing their flighty airborne dance at altitude, as if hoping to tempt an elusive sun to make an unguarded January appearance. And when it does, the sea suddenly acquires a blue all to itself, mirroring the sky. Though the town groans under the strain of its all-important tourist trade during the peak summer months, the locals are at peace with the frequently backed-up traffic and ice-cream overload; the noise and gridlock have become intrinsic, character-giving aspects of life in a town that lapses into hibernation for half of each year.

While there will be those low in sentiment who insist all water looks the same, you won't find many dwellers or regulars to St Ives in agreement. Just like your cat, which from a distance might resemble any other of its breed and age, the subtlest differences are all that matter to its owner. The bay's seabed steers the water currents in ways which cause the light to dart capriciously, as if just for our bedazzlement. The sea, as Iris Murdoch patiently unfolds in her bewitching book of 1978, *The Sea, The Sea*, is a place many gravitate to, either when contemplating retirement, a family holiday or, as is the case with Murdoch's main protagonist (an egocentric memoir writer), as a place where self-indulgent fantasy can gush out at whatever rate it feels the need to.

Today, if you stand alone somewhere along the craggy shoreline, or higher up on a surfaced path anywhere along the Lizard peninsula, you might imagine the first hesitant crackle Marconi heard as he began his intrepid wireless experiments back in 1901. The twin towers of the Lizard Lighthouse face confidently out to sea, overseeing what is still a hugely busy shipping lane, with its intermittent commotion carrying over the distance to the shore.

From this most southerly mainland point, visitors might allow their ears to pick up the multitude of frequencies available to them: the foot-jarring waves, thumping unremittingly at its most exposed crannies, and the welcome moments of reprieve in between. The eagle-eyed might spot an infrequent

MINDFULNESS EXERCISE

SEE THE SEA, HEAR THE WEIR

When the opportunity arises, head to the sea, to an active weir or large waterway. Take just a pair of binoculars, a sandwich and a good book. Imagine you are temporary custodian to this stretch of water. Settle down, shielded from any rude breeze that threatens to tug you back to reality. A bench set off from a coastal pathway could be ideal too, especially if your eye-line is unbroken by human busyness and your ears not often abraded by reminders of modern mundanity. You're here to savour the spectacle of water and to tune in to a soundscape of which you have just become the smallest part.

Once you've found an ideal spot to survey the beauty of your surroundings, close your eyes and slowly switch attention to your sense of smell: don't enquire or catalogue, just notice. As you take in longer breaths, one particular odour may strike you more acutely – allow it to steer you somewhere new, however removed from your present reality. Focus on the sounds that ride pillion to these smells, which may be a curious hybrid of natural and manufactured.

Begin to focus more on the sounds that are melding together: two distinct breeze artefacts perhaps – one by your ankles, the other nearer the shoreline; or three different wave artefacts – waves thundering onto the rocks, the *hushhhhhh* of the tide coming in, and the higher-pitched, more rapid hiss as the sea retreats. You are creating a vista of sound in your mind's ear, a safe, serene place. The following day, or week, why not revisit your sojourn to the seaside – sound memories will live on indefinitely if you reconnect with them from time to time – or better still, return to the same spot and top up your personal attachment to this rather special place.

razorbill, or notice the crazy dash of a sparrow hawk as the wind nibbles manically at their ears. Even in the cutting winter air there is a curious sensation of sounds to store away for future use, perhaps as you sit in your bath tub later, slowly bringing back the warmth to your extremities and tasting odd fragments of melting salt.

DREAMSCAPES

Dreams and daydreams are perhaps not unlike ghosts – we may be sceptical of what they amount to, and yet at times they can be surprisingly persuasive. Our dreams, whatever they amount to, however unintelligible they seem, always belong to us, and some can serve as a useful starting point for a meditation.

WE CANNOT HARVEST A DREAM while in the moment, though some people are convinced they are able to alter its course, avert a disaster or reroute an unhappy ending. If you make a point of writing down the more positive, distinctive fragments of a dream you can recall, you may well find familiar or recurring elements which can inspire you at unexpected points during your waking day. For me, sound is intrinsic to my dreaming. Imagined sounds – not often 'real' music, more a mishmash of vocalizations and sound textures that I can't quite put my finger on – add another dimension to the inspiring impossibility of what I'm experiencing.

Whether or not you experience sound in your dreams, it certainly helps to become aware of the physical environment your dream occupies, if indeed you feel it has one. This could be a pastoral outlook, such as a misty valley or paradisiacal landscape, an epic alpine vista or scorched wasteland. In my case, the setting is often a fantastical space-movie type scene, which usually comes as something of a surprise, since I've only made it to the end of a couple of such films in my entire life.

The details of a dream, its meaning and references to more deep-seated emotional states or issues, of course move into the realm of a qualified dream analyst or psychologist, who with the advantage of experience and context may be able to infer certain helpful interpretations. And yet, we don't need expert analysis simply to recall the ambience or poetic slant of a dream; its figurative reality or random elements won't necessarily mean anything in order to be valuable or transformative. With this haziest of recollections replanted in your mind, allow yourself to drift along a thought corridor; let it lead you wherever it wants to.

'Your vision will become clear only when
you can look into your own heart. Who looks outside,
dreams; who looks inside, awakes.'

CARL JUNG (1875–1961)
SWISS PSYCHOLOGIST

If you hear music or other sounds in your dream, these can be worthwhile vehicles for a meditation, too. Perhaps you use a meditation track to get off to sleep, which could then find its way morphed into your dream as a kind of soundtrack. Being alive to the idea of imagined sound is being receptive to an ethereal state of being, and surely mindfulness is partly about being open to transformation and transportation.

NIGHTSCAPES

At night, some feel the world reveals its alter-ego. It's the time we, along with many other animals and plants, take the opportunity to rest. But we also tend to associate night with darker, mysterious happenings, when the world's level of malevolence experiences an unmistakable spike.

WRITERS OF HORROR MOVIES, ghost stories and murder mysteries typically reserve their more spine-tingling scenes for the night, perhaps punctuating the darkness with a blood-curdling fox's scream or creaking coffin lid, backlit by a shadowy, watchful moon. Such scenes are commonly soaked in an eerie silence, or perhaps feature a harpsichord tinkling menacingly in the background. Night-time is when most of us are tucked up safely asleep in our beds, but we can be confident that bad things will be happening elsewhere, perhaps even next door. The boogieman is a night-time myth, as is

Dracula; werewolves are depicted howling at the moon, and the sound an owl makes is by implication haunting or symbolic of something ominous. Pending doom somehow feels more palpable when cast in the dead of night, and the darkness of the night sky is often interpreted metaphorically as a darkness of mood or depression.

But these are all nonsensical stereotypes – things that go 'bump' in the night, the stuff of fantasists and scaremongers, whose currency is the macabre, preying on our irrationality and vulnerability. Negative connotations, superstitions and apparitions tend to be self-serving and often border on the ridiculous. Halloween, and other icons of nocturnal entertainment, such as haunted castles or ghost trains in fairgrounds, have become something of an industry, capitalizing on a near-fear threshold that has become normalized by the time we are toddlers. We shrug these things off as harmless fun; perhaps also we reason that it's no bad thing to be afraid of the dark?

To caricature the night as unwittingly complicit in all this nocturnal mayhem is to diminish our capacity to marvel at its unique beauty and meditative positivity. The night is not a doom-laden blanket of evil that falls from the sky, nor just a convenient mechanism for drawing a line under another day, but a time for us to reflect positively on that day. The night has special mystical qualities and is for some loaded with spiritual meaning. Beyond the cliche of owls hooting and the clangour of partygoers drifting home, what does the night *sound* like to you?

MINDFULNESS EXERCISE

TAKE IN THE NIGHT AIR

Find a safe, familiar place, which you associate with wholly positive thoughts. Perhaps you enjoy a shaded corner of your garden or favourite spot on a shared roof space. Sit for a while alone on a summer's day, reading a book or simply enjoying cloud formations. This will be the place you return to at night. For now, breathe in the air and soak up your surroundings; notice the shadows on the fence, or the heat shimmering up from the paving stones, but refrain from calculating what is causing what. Smell what there is to smell, be it a far-off BBQ or a nearby sage plant, but again avoid analysis. Close your eyes and slowly tune in to what you can hear; it might be distant laughter or a wooden gate creaking on its hinges.

When you return to this same spot, make it as late as possible, when there is little likelihood of being disturbed. Follow a similar order of noticing your surroundings, first visually, then nasally and finally by closing your eyes and drinking in whatever sounds drift towards you. It is this nocturnal sound world that I'm guessing you'll remember most vividly. Don't search or wait for sounds to arrive, or anticipate specific night noises, but draw yourself into this pre-sleep world. Whatever motivates you to leave, perhaps fifteen minutes later, is for you to decide; you might be feeling chilly or drowsy.

When, finally, you are in bed, close your eyes and allow the sound sensation of your night-time meditation to return if it chooses to. Feel the security of your room, the warmth in your toes and the softness of your pillows. Let the ambience of your somnolent meditation live on in your mind; give it permission not to make sense.

SKYSCAPES

Flight magnifies our perspective, not just on the enormity of space, or on how whole continents seem to segue into huge masses of ocean, but on our own lives. No inch of sky is quite like any other; it's the ultimate vantage point from where to catch sight of ourselves scurrying around like ants.

THERE'S SOMETHING ETERNALLY ENCHANTING about flight. No amount of facts or physics about wind speed, leading edges or lift will ever diminish the sense of impossibility I always feel when I sit in a plane. This high-altitude view of the world just compounds my sense of awe; it has done little to further my understanding of it. Realizing how beautiful even the most industrial town can appear from the air alters our conception of what beauty is. It occurs to me that the opposite trajectory does this equally when, for example, we look in microscopic detail at something as mundane as a blade of grass at 100 × magnification.

If you ever get the chance, go tandem paragliding, preferably somewhere where you will get to see a wide variety of terrain moving in slow-motion beneath you like a patched quilt. My trip to the Babadağ mountain, near Ölüdeniz in southern Turkey, took an unexpected turn when I decided to suppress my fear of heights and, in a moment of unguarded bravura, leap off the top of this 2,000-metre hulk of a mountain. The hour-long dirt track in a Jeep was scary enough, chicaning around the mountain's periphery, driven by one of the pilots who I swear didn't look at the track ahead of him once during the entire sky-bound journey. The sun had swelled into a massive caldron-red disc at this dusky hour. We looked down onto an implausibly small beach landing, the size of a postage stamp, and surveyed a row of teethy cliffs chiselled into the sea.

I won't forget the chilling words muttered quietly to me by my seasoned pilot ten seconds before our epic leap of faith: 'When I say run, run… or we will both *die*.' I ran, eyes closed, into a warm, silent, breathy updraft. An awkward shuffle into my seat led to a shriek of exaltation, relief, pride or perhaps shock at this oddly meaningful achievement. 'I'll do some silly stuff over the sea first, if you want, then we can just fly.' The silly stuff involved nose dives, loop-the-loops and other acts of wanton craziness, much of which went by as if in a trance, and I even had a go at flying the thing myself. Before long, just as he'd promised, we settled the pace to the gentlest of glides and flew in complete silence for nearly an hour, floating as if on a magic carpet.

I say silence, but the sound of the forty-foot wing slicing through the air, wing tips arching the horizon, generated a considerable amount of commotion as the wind picked up into sporadic gusts. Within this hour, I recall a ten-minute sliver of perfection; an extraordinary meditation. I tracked the horizon, not wanting to blink for fear of missing out on my peripheral vision; a large bird then glided in – either it was slipstreaming us or just amused at the spectacle of two helmeted men squeezed into what looked like a banana-shaped sleeping bag. Quickly a new kind of sound-energy filled my ears – the inward tide hastening landwards and the whirring of barely visible frisbees darting hauntingly overhead. The feathery thud of our landing seemed inversely proportional to the airborne energy we had expended during the flight.

If I close my eyes and conjure up the spectacle of my first engineless flight, what returns to me is my aromatic meditation, the sound of the sky hurrying towards darkness overhead and the beach where it would all come to an elegant full-stop zooming in at an exponential speed. *Owning* my fear felt so important, rather than trying to overcome it, while at the same time allowing the dusty scent of the thermal air to envelop me. It was dusk, and yet the world's celestial clockwork was already well underway; I could almost hear the firmament ticking as I bounced along the sand, filled with glee, dragging my flaccid wing behind me, like some war-weary hero returning victorious from an epic battle in the skies. My head was brimming over with potent sounds. The mysticism of the sky had become redolent with meaning; I sensed a curious kinship with it. What better way to connect the splendour of nature, the simple gift of mindfulness and the transforming power of meditation?

RESOURCES

Cheung, S., Han, E., Kushki, A., Anagnostou, E., Biddiss, E., *Biomusic: An Auditory Interface for Detecting Physiological Indicators of Anxiety in Children. Front Neurosci.* 2016;10:401. Published August 30 2016. https://www.ncbi.nlm.nih.gov/pmc/articles/PMC5003931. Accessed August 29 2019.

Gagliano, M., *Thus Spoke the Plant; A Remarkable Journey of Groundbreaking Scientific Discoveries and Personal Encounters with Plants*, North Atlantic Books, 2018

Gilbert, Dr Paul, YouTube Video https://youtube/Gm_PEFYgnus. Accessed August 2 2019.

'Baby cries shorten our reaction time', Professor Morten Kringelbach of MindLab, posted on sciencenordic.com. Accessed July 25 2019.

Schopenhauer, Arthur, *The World as Will and Representation, Cambridge University Press, 2014*

Tanner, M., *Mindfulness in Music*, Leaping Hare Press, 2018

Tanner, M., *The Mindful Pianist*, Faber Music, 2016

It's True – You Really Should Talk to Your Plants, Colleen Vanderlinden https://www.thespruce.com/should-you-talk-to-your-plants-3972298. Accessed July 18 2019.

Watkins, H., *Musical Vitalities: Ventures in a Biotic Aesthetics of Music*, University of Chicago Press, 2018

Useful Websites

American Tinnitus Association: www.ata.org

British Tinnitus Association: www.tinnitus.org.uk

INDEX

acoustics 41–9
advertisements 54, 59
aeroacoustics 44–5
AIHO 58
aircraft 44
algorithms 48, 49
ambient sound 8, 58
anechoic chamber 78
Anthropocene epoch 53–4
anxiety 47–8, 74
archaeoacoustics 44
Arctic voyage 61–2
Aristotle 41
artificial intelligence (AI) 48–9
ASMR 56, 58–9, 61
ASMRtist 59
association 64–6, 69

baby crying 47, 115
bathing 18–20
Bayeux Tapestry 101
Beatles 72
bells 9, 21
binaural beats therapy 87–8
biomusic 14, 47–8, 96–7
birds 27, 29, 34, 132
blissfulness 52–4, 55
brain 12, 24, 33–4, 63–4
brain massage 58
brass instruments 44
breathing 9, 24–9, 109, 112
Buddha 73
Buddhism 9, 14, 51, 110, 111

camouflage 116
Carlyle, Thomas 96
cats 67–8, 130
cave paintings 44
chakras 110
chanting 15, 108–13
chronobiology 14

cityscapes 120–5
cognitive behavioural therapy (CBT) 84–5
coin spinning 69
Cole, Nat King 94
commodification 54–6
communication 27, 29
compassion 68, 83–7, 100, 114
compassionate focus therapy (CFT) 83–7
concert halls 42, 43–4
Cooke, Lucy 115–16
Crumb, George 97

Darwin, Charles 98, 99, 116
Dawkins, Richard 116
deceit 115–17
deep listening 37–41
direction of sound 33–4
dis-ease/disease 15–16
distance 34–5
dolphins 34–5, 43
Doyle, Arthur Conan 126
dreamscapes 132–4
dynamic meditation 72

ears 31, 32–7, 42
echolocation 44
emotion 45, 48, 63–6, 108, 109, 110
entrainment 14–15

Forster, E.M. 74
frequency 32–3, 43
    binaural beats 87
    infrasonic 43
    ultrasonic 43, 44

Gagliano, Monica 97
Galileo Galilei 41, 42
Generation Anxious 74
Gershwin, George and Ira 107

Gilbert, Paul 85, 86
Glennie, Evelyn 38
Great Acceleration 54
greenscapes 125–8
Gurmukhi 109

habituation 90
headphones 25, 34, 44
    noise-cancelling 78–9
healing 14–17
hearing aids 44
hearing impairment 38
hearing range 31–2
Hertz 43
Hinduism 73, 110, 112
Hong Kong 127–8
house plants 28
human echolocation 44
hydrodynamics 14

incantations 113–14
infrasonic frequencies 43
Inness, George 95–6

Jones, Tom 94
Jung, Carl 133

King, Martin Luther 65
Kringelbach, Morten 47
Kundalini yoga 109

laughter 16–17
lexical entrainment 14–15
listening 37–41
lying 115–17

mantra 72, 108–11
measuring distance 34–5
meditation soundtrack 21, 60, 69
memory 9, 64, 104–6
Mersenne, Marin 42
Monet, Claude 95–6
monkey mind 73
moon 79–80
Mother Teresa of Calcutta 80

moths 75–7
Murdoch, Iris 130
Mussorgsky, Modest 94

Nash, Johnny 94
nature 80, 81, 94–101, 125–8
nightscapes 134–6
notifications 57

Om 111–13

panning 34
paragliding 137–9
Pärt, Arvo 36
phonetics 107
phonology 108
physics 14, 41–4
pitch 32–3, 34, 113
plants 28, 97–8
Plato 84
Pollock, Jackson 95–6
primates 73, 117
programme music 96
psychoacoustics 46–7
public spaces 35, 42, 43–4
Pythagoras 41

raked seating 42
resonance 10–13, 15–16, 33
running a bath 18–19

Sain-Saëns, Camille 95
Sanskrit 109, 110, 114
Sat Kriya meditation 111
Sat Nam mantra 111
Satipatthana 73
Schopenhauer, Arthur 97, 98–9
Scientific Revolution 42
seascapes 129–32
self-compassion 68, 84, 86–7, 114
silence 21, 74, 77–83, 123
singing bowls 14, 15
skyscapes 137–9
snakes 114
sonic fingerprint 104

sound engineers 34
sound physics 41–4
soundscapes 26, 129
spectrum analysis 37, 44
speech recognition 106
Strauss, Richard 101
subtle body 110

tapestry 100–1
Thunberg, Greta 74
Tibetan Buddhism 14, 111
Tibetan Ting-Sha bells 21
Tibetan singing bowls 14, 15
timbre 9, 32–3, 35–7
time 40
timer 21
tinnitus 88–91
    self-healing 90–1
tone quality see timbre
tone of voice 114–15
transcendental meditation 72
transduction 43
tweeters 43
tympanum (see also ears) 32, 42, 75

ultrasonic frequencies 43, 44

Vaughan Williams, Ralph 94
vibration 10, 12–13, 15, 38, 42, 98,
    109
Vitruvius 42
Vivaldi, Antonio 94
volume 31–2, 33–4, 89

water 17–18, 40, 130
Watkins, Holly 97, 98–9
wave motion 41, 42–3
whale noises 60, 97
white noise 8, 89
wind instruments 44
woofers 43
Woolf, Virginia 58
Wordsworth, William 123

yoga 109, 110, 112

Zen 51, 81

PRAISE FOR *Mindfulness in Music*, 2018

◆

'*Mindfulness in Music* is both informative and
thought-provoking - a fascinating read on many levels.'
JULIAN LLOYD WEBBER

'Mark Tanner has written a mindfulness manifesto for music'
BBC RADIO 3: MUSIC MATTERS

'Peppered with intriguing exercises and motivational quotes'
BBC MUSIC MAGAZINE

DEDICATION

◆

For Gily

ACKNOWLEDGEMENTS

◆

I'd like to acknowledge the non-intrusive assistance, careful editing and thoughtful contributions from Joanna Bentley, Imogen Palmer and Monica Perdoni at Leaping Hare Press.

Many of my ideas, experiences and adventures in the world of sound have been shared ones — it's interesting that the simplest, most inconspicuous vibrations of the air take on an altogether new and more vivid meaning when they are experienced with others. A nod or half smile is often all that's needed, even between two complete strangers, to acknowledge the common currency of a rather beautiful, unexpected sound. I thank my fellow musicians, family and friends for their welcome off-the-cuff insights; in particular, my partner Gillian Poznansky, who I can always rely on for an honest response to my creations.

Following on from *Mindfulness in Music*, *Mindfulness in Sound* has given me an opportunity to indulge and probe a little more deeply into the splendour of sound and its astonishing capacity to shape a moment in time. Naturally, the reader will come across topic areas in this earlier book that I've not felt the need to revisit here, despite some inevitable resonances; indeed the points of convergence have been immensely stimulating to prise open.